Change Your Life in 7 Days

Also by Paul McKenna

I Can Make You Thin

I Can Make You Thin: 90-Day Success Journal

I Can Make You Sleep

I Can Make You Confident

Quit Smoking Today Without Gaining Weight

I Can Make You Happy

I Can Make You Rich

I Can Mend Your Broken Heart
(with *Hugh Willbourn*)

The Hypnotic World of Paul McKenna

Change Your Life in
7 DAYS

Paul McKenna, PhD

Edited by Michael Neil

STERLING
New York

STERLING
New York

An Imprint of Sterling Publishing
387 Park Avenue South
New York, NY 10016

First US edition 2013.

ISBN 978-1-4027-6573-5

Distributed in Canada by Sterling Publishing
c/o Canadian Manda Group, 165 Dufferin Street
Toronto, Ontario, Canada M6K 3H6

For information about custom editions, special sales, and premium
and corporate purchases, please contact Sterling Special Sales at
800-805-5489 or specialsales@sterlingpublishing.com.

Manufactured in the United States of America

2   4   6   8   10   9   7   5   3

www.sterlingpublishing.com

To my parents, who gave me more than I realized

I would like to thank all of my colleagues, clients, and students who have contributed to this book.

I would especially like to thank Richard Bandler, Michael Neill, Michael Breen, Diana Beaver, Doug Young, Clare Staples, Mike Osborne, and Paul Duddridge.

CHANGE YOUR LIFE DVD AND CD

Your mind is like a computer—it has its own software that helps you to organize your thinking and behavior. Having worked with all sorts of people with different problems over many years, I have learned that almost all problems stem from the same cause—negative programs running in the unconscious mind.

This book comes with a powerful mind-programming DVD and hypnosis CD that will fill your unconscious mind with positive thoughts and feelings.

THE DVD

There are seven different sessions that each last for a few minutes. Each session builds on the one before, so most start by repeating some of the techniques from the previous one. It's a really good idea to use the DVD at the start of each day to program your mind to be in a peak state. We can't control everything that ever happens to us, but when you approach each day in a highly resourceful state you can easily handle any challenges that occur.

In each session I personally coach you through various visualization exercises, giving you time to think about things that will empower you and help you to focus upon achieving your goals.

THE CD

As you listen to the hypnosis CD you become absorbed into a natural state of deep relaxation for about twenty-five minutes. I will reprogram your unconscious mind to help you become happier, more confident, creative, and more focused upon achieving your goals.

Each time you listen, it will become easier to relax and the positive programming will go deeper into your mind. The latest research into the effectiveness of hypnosis and similar techniques has shown that repeated listening to this CD has many benefits, including enhanced emotional equilibrium and better health.

You don't have to believe it—just use it!

There is a special Change Your Life in 7 Days—Positive Software for the Mind CD included with this book.

Warning

Do not listen to the CD while driving or operating heavy machinery or if you suffer from epilepsy or clinical depression. If in doubt, consult your doctor.

Contents

Introduction   3

1. Day One
   Who Are You, Really?   17

2. Day Two
   A User's Manual for Your Brain   45

3. Day Three
   The Power of a Positive Perspective   85

4. Day Four
   Dreamsetting   119

5. Day Five
   Healthy Foundations   157

6. Day Six
   Creating Money   191

7. Day Seven
   Happily Ever After   235

Conclusion
Changing Your Life, One Week at a Time   265

Change Your Life in
7 DAYS

Introduction

You hold in your hands a book that has the power to change your life forever.

Does that seem like an outlandish claim? So many of the people I've guided to achieving their desires started out wondering how it is possible and ended up astounding themselves. Now it's your turn. Don't underestimate the power of the system in this book. I promise you—it will change your life!

Success and happiness are not accidents that just "happen" to some people and not to others—they are predictable results created by deliberate ways of thinking and acting, ways that I'll be sharing with you over the next seven days. As the saying goes, success is all about luck—ask any failure!

Can I Really Change My Life in 7 Days?

People are always amazed in my seminars when we cure lifelong phobias in a few minutes, or clear up supposedly "deep-seated issues" in just a few days. But most people can think of a time when their lives changed in just a few moments. Perhaps it was getting a new piece of important information, or meeting a special someone and knowing that your life would never be the same.

> *"Whether you think you can or you think you can't you're probably right."*
> HENRY FORD

Here is the reason why change can happen so quickly:

The changes that matter most are more often changes in perception than changes in the world outside us.

And we can change the way we perceive the world in a heartbeat.

In fact, the myth that it takes a long time to change has only been around for about a hundred years, when Freudian analysis became the dominant influence in the treatment of psychosomatic illness. What makes this point of view ironic is that psychoanalysis isn't really about changing people—it's more to do with helping them gain a deeper understanding of why they are the way they are. In my work, understanding is the booby prize!

Sometimes even a small change can make a huge difference. For example, imagine you and another person are driving along two straight roads, stretching side by side off into the infinite distance. Now imagine that one of those roads shifts even a tiny bit away from the other. At first the difference might seem imperceptible. But over time, that small change in direction would take you to an entirely different destination from the other person.

The techniques contained in *Change Your Life in 7 Days* are state of the art, offering not only the latest software but also a whole new operating system for your body and mind.

Each day, you will make tiny changes, changes that may be imperceptible to you at first. But as you continue moving forward, you will begin to realize just how far you have already come and just how much you have changed.

Let's face it—if you do virtually anything consistently for seven days it will change you. What makes this system different is that many of the techniques you will be learning as you read will go on working, helping you long after you stop using them. Over the next seven days the actions you take will set up a wave of change in your life that will in turn affect many other areas of your life, which in turn affect others. Just as an oil tanker takes a little while to start moving, it becomes difficult to stop once it builds up sufficient momentum.

For centuries people had thought it was impossible to run a four-minute mile. Then on May 6, 1954, Roger Bannister did what all great pioneers do—he made the impossible happen.

> "What is now proved was once impossible."
> WILLIAM BLAKE

I met Dr. Bannister and we talked about how amazing it was that within a year of him breaking the four-minute mile, thirty-seven other people around the world had done so as well. In the following year, an incredible *three hundred runners* broke through that previously impenetrable barrier.

The finest minds of the age had believed it was impossible to do, and their beliefs became a self-fulfilling prophecy. (Some noted scientists actually suggested that the human body would *explode* if pushed to go faster than a four-minute mile!)

It took only one counter-example—one person

proving that what they had previously thought could not be done was possible—for everyone else to tap into that possibility within themselves.

The human mind generalizes as a learning principle. For example, as a child you learn how a door opens and closes. Your mind then generalizes that information to apply to all doors everywhere.

This works equally well whether the lessons are useful or painful. Over the next seven days, we are going to dismantle many of the negative generalizations you have made about the world and build positive new ones.

My Story

I became interested in all things self-improvement shortly after I left school. It didn't take long for me to read nearly every self-help book, try every technique, and apply everything I was learning to my own life. As a result, my life changed dramatically for the better. In fact, since I began using the techniques I am about to share with you, I quickly noticed an improvement in my confidence, finances, career, and the way people treated me. I became wealthy, famous, and my life became infinitely more glamorous than it was before—all in a short space of time. All of the best techniques that I used to create the life I live today are contained in the book you now hold in your hands!

My purpose in life, and the goal of this book, is to help you get greater control of yourself and your life. Since 1985, I have been working on a revolutionary self-improvement system that will work for everyone. The unique success-conditioning system you are about to learn has now been perfected—you will begin making profound changes within the very first day.

Best of all, you can relax—it's very easy, and you don't have to have any previous experience or skill. In fact, if you can close your eyes, talk to yourself and others, and move your body, you can control your thinking and behavior, and ultimately you can live the life of your dreams. All you have to do is follow my instructions step by step, even if at times you're not sure you're doing it right. Together, we are going to design and install "positive software" for your mind!

The Power of Now

This is an exciting time in history. Our world is transforming every day. The scientific and techno-logical transformations and breakthroughs that are taking place all around us are increasing at exponential rates. We, as a human race, are connecting over great distances, exploring and reshaping our world. Journeys that used to take months are now made in hours; calculations that used to take years are now done in minutes. The question is not will your life change—the question is what will it change *into*?

Right now we live in a digital information age. Faxes, mobile telephones, computers, and satellite technology, unthinkable even fifty years ago, are now considered a normal part of modern-day twenty-first-century life. Something happens on one side of the world and we can watch it on our television screens moments later. Global communications systems can connect mind to mind like nerve cells in a huge global brain. Wherever it is we are going, we are going there fast!

We stand on the threshold of an enormous leap in our evolution, and I believe that the next great stage in human development will be a move out of the information age and into a new time where people will begin to develop their inner resources. I call this time the age of *psycho-technology*—a time when we will begin to unleash the amazing powers and inner abilities that we are all born with. I see the understanding and practice of *psycho-technology* as being like having an owner's manual for your brain.

Unfortunately, most people spend more time learning to work their DVD player than they do their own mind. By taking the next week to read and practice the exercises in this book, you are marking yourself out as different from the 98 percent of people who, to quote Winston Churchill, "stumble over the truth from time to time but quickly get up, dust themselves off, and move on as if nothing happened."

In this book, you'll discover the techniques that have helped many people break through their limitations and release their true potential. Together, we are going to program your mind to make you a happier, more confident, and more powerful person.

Getting Started

Before you begin on this journey into your true potential, I'd like you to stop and consider this:

What would it be like if you woke up one morning and a miracle had happened—your life had become exactly what you wanted it to be?

Do it now. Stop and vividly imagine it.

- How would you know that the miracle had taken place?

- What would you see?

- What would you hear?

- What would you feel inside?

- What changes would have happened in your career?

- In your relationships?

- Your finances?

- Your health?

As you use the ideas and practice the techniques you will learn from this book, you are going to make these dreams come true.

Simply relax, read, and allow the ideas and exercises in the book to take root.

Just as a gardener plants seeds and patiently waits for them to grow, every time you work with this book, you're planting positive suggestions in your mind that will grow into powerful new ways to operate the world's most advanced bio-computer—your brain!

Even though you can achieve dramatic results in

> "People are always
> blaming circumstances
> for what they are. I don't
> believe in circumstances.
> The people who get
> ahead in this world
> are the people who get
> up and look for the
> circumstances they want,
> and if they can't find
> them, make them."
>
> GEORGE BERNARD SHAW

your very first week, you may want to return to the book several times in the first few months. It is vitally important to do the exercises in order to get the kind of results you want. No single technique is a magic pill for success but when you practice them again and again they will become second nature to you.

Whatever you achieve in the next ten years will be the result of what you do now—as the saying goes, if you keep doing what you've always done you'll just get more of what you've already got. But you do have the power to make an incredible difference to your life. And it starts right here. . . .

The Difference That Makes the Difference

Many people begin a self-help book or personal training program but quit halfway through. They convince themselves that it's too hard, or they don't have what it takes. Here's the problem with that approach:

If you don't take control of your life, someone else will.

Now, I know responsibility isn't a very popular word these days. Billions of dollars change hands each year as people literally "pass the buck" on whose fault it is that their coffee was too hot, their body was too weak, or their dog was too poorly trained.

But another way of thinking about responsibility is that it is really about control. Do you want to control your life, or hand over that control to other people—your family, the media, or even society in general? Do you want to be the master of your fate or the victim of your circumstances?

Taking responsibility is taking control of those parts of your life that are within your control, while letting go of trying to control what is not.

It's easy to blame your parents, employers, or the government for your problems, but until you decide to see yourself as responsible for your situation then you don't have any power to change it. All great achievers know that taking responsibility is the first step toward having a successful and fulfilling life.

Dr. Stephen R. Covey describes it like this:

> *"When you pick up one end of the stick,*
> *you pick up the other. Therefore, if*

> *you decide to take responsibility for*
> *your circumstances, you automatically*
> *tap into the power to change them."*

When I share these ideas in my seminars, occasionally a participant will say to me, "Does that mean that if I'm walking across the road and I get run over it's my fault?"

The answer is simple—taking responsibility is not the same as taking the blame. You are not responsible for the hand you have been dealt, but it is always up to you how you play it.

Stop for a moment and imagine what it would be like to take responsibility for your life—to have the power to make choices and changes in every area of your life. To be in control of your finances, your relationships, and your sense of well-being. To be at peace with those things that are not in your control and in full command of those that are.

If you like what you are imagining, make the decision right now to take responsibility for your life at a whole new level. The more I work with people who achieve astounding results, the more I am inspired by the words of W. H. Murray:

> *"Until one is committed, there is hesitancy,*
> *the chance to draw back, always*

ineffectiveness. Concerning all acts of initiative (and creation), there is one elementary truth the ignorance of which kills countless ideas and splendid plans: that the moment one definitely commits oneself, then providence moves too. A whole stream of events issues from the decision, raising in one's favor all manner of unforeseen incidents, meetings and material assistance, which no man could have dreamt would have come his way."

Are you committed? Are you ready to take back your power? Are you willing to make this book important enough to follow the simple instructions that will change your life? Even if you're not convinced at first, it is important to realize that you can succeed in spite of yourself! It all happens one chapter at a time. . . .

How to Use This Book

This book is laid out in seven chapters—seven key lessons that will guide you from wherever you are in the direction of your most deeply felt values and most fondly hoped-for dream. There is also a CD, which contains a powerful mind-programming technique that will fill your mind with positive suggestions and prepare your brain for the valuable information you will be receiving in that day's reading.

You can listen to the CD during the day or as you are going to sleep. Do not listen to it while operating machinery; listen only when you can safely relax. That is all you need to do to succeed!

In just seven days, you will join the ranks of those people who are so well programmed to succeed that they cannot help but be successful at what they do. You will be able to handle whatever challenges life offers you with a sense of ease and confidence. Your journey will begin in the next chapter, as you discover who you are becoming and uncover your true potential to become the person you really want to be. . . .

DAY ONE

Who Are You, Really?

Discover your true potential and become
the person you really want to be

IMAGINE YOU WOKE UP ONE DAY in a land populated almost entirely by giants. At first you would no doubt be terrified, and the deafening roar of loud noises and the uncomfortable sinking feeling when you fell would stick with you for a lifetime. After a time, you would realize that many of the giants seemed friendly, and that one giant in particular was taking a particular interest in your safety and well-being.

Then imagine that one day, for no reason whatsoever, the giant you had learned to trust completely yelled at you, threatened you, even hit you. How could you ever feel safe again in a land of giants? There must be some laws of the land or rules that you could learn to help you survive. . . .

One day, you meet some other little people. They appear to be like you, and in their company, you instantly feel more secure. Some of them claim to know the laws of the land, and they share them with you. Combined with the insight you've gained from observing the giants and listening to them teach you in their booming God-like voices, you begin to figure out what you need to do and not do to stay safe.

Do as you are told. It's easier to get along if you go along. Don't cry. Don't fight. Study hard. Get a job. Do as you are told. Get married. Have children to support you in your old age. Do as you are told.

The list grows longer as your once tiny body grows larger (nurtured no doubt by the special food produced in the land of the giants), and eventually you come to realize that there are no giants left.

And then one day you wake up, and there is a tiny little creature staring up at you. She has awakened in a land of giants. And because you love her, you begin to teach her everything you've learned about how to survive in this land of giants.

And so, the cycle continues. . . .

The Power of Brainwashing

During the Korean civil war of the late 1950s, the Chinese Koreans successfully converted an unprecedented number of American POWs to the "religion" of communism. They didn't do it through threat of torture or even promise of reward—they did it by simply changing the soldiers' self-image.

What the Chinese understood was that our behavior is a direct result of the person we believe we are—our self-image. Think of it like a loop—we are constantly confirming to ourselves that we are the person we think we are, but the system we use to interpret our behavior and feedback is our own self-image. It's a catch-22.

Have you listened to the morning programming session on the CD yet?

If you really want to change your life in the next seven days, you can—and you don't need to spend thousands of dollars doing it. Just listen to the CD twice a day, follow along with the exercises in this book, and you are already on your way to a whole new experience of living!

So the Chinese interrupted the loop. You might have thought it would be a big task reprogramming men who had been highly trained only to give their name, rank, and serial number, but they did it bit by bit—one small piece at a time.

During an interrogation, prisoners were persuaded to make one or two mildly anti-American or pro-communist statements. (For example, "The United States is not perfect," or, "In a communist country, there is less unemployment and crime.") Once these apparently minor statements had been extracted, the prisoner would then be asked to define exactly how the United States was not perfect. When he was worn down and weary, he would then be asked to sign his name to the list of reasons he had come up with.

Later, the prisoner would be made to read his list in a discussion group with other prisoners. The Chinese would then broadcast his name and list of reasons during an anti-American radio broadcast not only to his own camp but to all the other North Korean POW camps and the rest of the American forces in South Korea as well.

Suddenly, the prisoner found himself labeled as a collaborator, someone who participated in "the kind of behavior that helped the enemy." When fellow prisoners asked why he had done it, he couldn't claim he had been tortured. After all, it had just been what he had said and signed himself.

Psychological research has shown that human beings can only tolerate a certain amount of discrepancy between their thoughts and their behavior.

Like anyone unaware of the power of their own self-image, the prisoner felt he had to justify his actions in order to maintain consistency with his own internal sense of identity. He would say that what he said was true. In that moment his self-image changed. He now believed he was pro-communist, and his fellow prisoners reinforced his new identity by treating him differently. The loop was complete.

Before long, his desire to act consistently with his new self-image would drive him to collaborate with the Chinese even more, thereby further reinforcing his new self-image until he no longer even questioned if it was true.

What Is a Self-image?

Your self-image is the way you see yourself in your imagination. The reason your self-image is so powerful is because your behavior will almost never deviate from this internal map. It acts as a sort of self-fulfilling prophecy, telling you how to behave or perform to act consistently with the kind of person you think you are. Yet many people don't even realize they have an image of themselves until they look.

We've all met people who are attractive but who think of themselves as ugly—too fat or too thin or too old or too young. If you truly believe you are unattractive, you will unconsciously sabotage any attempts to make yourself appear attractive. Because you won't represent yourself at your best, people will inevitably find you unattractive and the prophecy is fulfilled.

Studies have shown that an extraordinary number of people who suddenly receive large sums of money through lottery wins or inheritance are likely to lose it again almost as quickly. Even people who earn their money are likely to lose it if what they are earning is more than they believe they are worth. They feel uncomfortable with the extra money, so they spend it, or lend it, or find some other way to get rid of it.

Celebrities whose stars rise too high too fast can also be brought back to earth by the gravitational pull of a limited self-image. In fact, so many celebrities suffer from self-destructive behavior brought on by feelings of unworthiness that psychologists have created a name for the pattern: Paradise Syndrome.

How you think of yourself also affects how *other people* feel about you. Because more than 90 percent of what we communicate is unconscious, the people around you are continually responding to your body language, tone of voice, and the emotional signals you are transmitting. Even if the words you use sound positive, you may well find yourself conveying one message verbally and a completely different message with your body language.

Here's the point:

You are constantly letting other people know how to treat you by the way you treat yourself.

In the book *The Mastery of Love*, Don Miguel Ruiz shares the analogy of living in a restaurant where food was plentiful. If someone came to the door and offered you a pizza but you'd have to let them abuse you for the rest of your life, you'd laugh in their face. But if you were living in the street and hadn't eaten for days and that same person made you that same offer, you'd be likely to consider it. We settle in life for what we feel we are worth—that is, we will never allow anyone to abuse us more than we abuse ourselves.

> "We seek the teeth that made the wounds."
> ANONYMOUS

Success and the Self-image

Unfortunately, while each failure reinforces the self-fulfilling prophecy of your negative self-image, your outer successes rarely change it for the better. No matter how much you have on the outside—bigger house, bigger car, more money—it will not ultimately satisfy you if you don't already feel good about yourself on the inside.

Over the years I have had the opportunity to meet and work with a large number of "successful" people. I am continually struck by how many of them create an outer veneer as a way of hiding personal feelings of inadequacy. For example, they project any number of things to compensate for a lack of inner self-worth, flaunting their wealth, status, intellectual achievement, physical strength, social connections, or moral "superiority" in an attempt to prove that they are not as worthless as they feel inside.

Sometimes it starts out with a little lie, or a small affectation, but over the years it develops into an entire outer persona that is the complete opposite of how they feel on the inside. They continually feel like a fraud, fearing that at any moment they are going to be "found out," and it will all be taken away from them. In fact, many people whom we consider in our culture to have everything are secret self-haters. I call this the "bling-bling factor"—the bigger the jewelry, the smaller the self-image.

However, the bling-bling factor is by no means exclusively a problem of the rich and famous. In fact, having worked with people from all walks of life, I have come to the conclusion that almost *everybody* is to some extent hiding or compensating for a part of themselves that they don't like.

For a long time I'd felt that if only I could be rich enough, or famous enough, or date lots of beautiful women, then I would feel better about myself. I had been a nerdy kid, and my solution to that was to affix a veneer of success to myself so that no one (including myself) would notice how inadequate I really felt.

Over a relatively short period of time, I worked incredibly hard at achieving and did very well. I became famous, made money, and created all the trappings of a glamorous life. My TV shows were a huge hit, I had more money than ever before, and a beautiful model girlfriend. Rock stars, movie stars, even royalty wanted me to work with them.

However, I kept thinking to myself, I have everything I have ever wanted—how come I still feel empty?

So How Is Your Self-image Formed?

While some of the earliest messages you got from your family were no doubt positive, many of them were not. Whether you were told you were a "stupid child," "ungrateful," or "clumsy," you soaked up all the negative suggestions along with whatever positive reinforcement came your way. A recent study revealed that the average American parent criticizes their child eight times for every one time they praise them.

When you start school, so many people are bigger than you and seem to know more than you do. A whole new world of problems comes your way. Teachers unwittingly de-genius you at school by their efforts to mold you. Your spontaneous childlike quality becomes dissipated in the race to shape you into an adult.

> "We are born princes, and the civilizing process makes us into frogs."
> ERIC BERNE

Just as you're getting the hang of it, puberty arrives. Hairs grow, body parts change size, and just being alive is embarrassing. Then of course there are those people around you with low self-esteem who covertly undermine you to make themselves feel better.

Research has shown that by the age of fourteen,

98 percent of children have a negative self-image. And it only gets worse. Irish author J. H. Brennan describes it like this:

"If there is one word which ably describes adolescence, that word is confusion. And the confusion is so strongly felt that it can easily impinge on your basic self-image. It's a sorry picture: small . . . helpless . . . powerless . . . dirty . . . socially unacceptable . . . inferior . . . confused— and in particularly bad cases, unloved and unwanted as well. And sorry though it is, the image was largely accurate when it was laid down—not by yourself, but by the actions and opinions of others. And at this stage, Nature played you the dirtiest trick imaginable. You grew up, but your self-image didn't. No wonder there are so many people who aren't achieving what they would like in their lives!"

As I related J. H. Brennan's words to my own life, I was able to recognize that my fundamental problem was a sense of powerlessness—deep down, I still saw myself as a nerdy, helpless child. Whatever sense of power I had in my life did not come from my authentic self, but was drawn solely from the reflected status I felt from my successful career, beautiful girlfriend, and financial resources.

From meeting and working with many famous and "successful" people I already knew how much of what they had achieved was to compensate for their feelings of inadequacy. It had never before occurred to me that I was one of them.

Once I got really clear on the content of my negative self-image, I knew it was time to make some fundamental changes. I had already made the decision to take responsibility for my life, so it was only a small step from there to take responsibility for how I chose to see myself. I resolved then and there to begin pursuing a new dream. I wanted to develop an approach to understanding and creating human excellence with a heart—not just success, but happiness and fulfillment as well. I was determined to find a way to "heal the nerd within!"

The Best Advice in the World

In the mid-1980s, John Opel, then chairman of IBM, gave a talk to an audience of Stanford MBAs.

In response to a request for his advice about how newly minted MBAs should embark on their careers, he said he would share one of his "secrets" for true success. As the eager young minds in the audience leaned forward, Opel whispered:

"Don't fake it!"

He paused and read the body language in the room. He then said, with great passion:

"No, really, I mean it!"

The room erupted in laughter. He went on to say that we are all smart enough and smooth enough to fake it and get away with it for a while, but eventually our faith in ourselves will be undermined, and with it our self-trust, self-respect, and self-esteem.

HERE IS TODAY'S KEY LESSON:

The reason you are not yet living the life of your dreams is that you are wasting so much of your time and energy hiding your negative self-image from the world.

When all your energy is going into maintaining the illusion of your projected self and hiding the image of your feared self from the world, the still, small voice of the authentic self—who you really are—can barely be heard.

But as you practice the exercises in today's lesson, you will begin to see yourself in a new light. You will learn to turn up the volume on that inner voice, to trust your gut, and to begin to follow the promptings of your own heart. And when you do that, your life will change forever!

The Three Selves

At our core is our authentic self—the reality of who and what we really are.

But piled on top of the real us—with all our weirdness, foibles, and unabashed "us"-ness—is that layer of shame, fear, and guilt, the person we're *afraid* we are, our negative self-image.

So in order to make sure people still like us, approve of us, and give us love and money, we pile yet ANOTHER layer on top of our feared self—the person we *pretend* to be.

This uppermost layer is, if we're very, very good pretenders, all others get to see of us. In fact, we struggle so valiantly to make sure no one sees that layer of liabilities we are afraid characterizes us, that we completely forget (sometimes for years at a time) that there's another, REAL self underneath all that.

When I first shared this model with one of my friends, she told me, "Oh, I get it! Our real selves are like diamonds, and as we grow up they get covered up in a lot of horseshit, so we put nail polish on top of the horseshit to try and make ourselves more attractive to the world. But if we spent a little bit of time digging away at the horseshit, people would see that we're really diamonds and we wouldn't need any nail polish!"

I probably would've put it a bit more like this:

As you begin to excavate your real self out from under who you're afraid you are and who you pretend to be (i.e., excavate the diamond out from under the horse manure covered in nail polish!), you get to shift positions from driven to driver. And when your real self is driving the bus, you get to have more ease, more fun, and more YOU in your life!

Getting to Know Your Selves

Let's take a closer look at the characteristics of the three selves as they relate to your own life. I will share with you some

> *"The unexamined life is not worth living."*
> SOCRATES

of my favorite questions for unmasking your pretend self, uncovering your negative self-image, or feared self, and unleashing your authentic self. Remember, there are no "right" answers—each question is simply designed to raise your awareness of what stops you from living from your authentic self:

a. Your Pretend Self: Who You Pretend to Be

Your pretend self is the image you project into the world. Often, this image is based less on how you really are than on covering over how you are afraid you are. Ask and answer the following questions:

- **How do you like to be seen?**

- **Which aspects of your personality do you hope people notice first?**

- **What is it most important that everyone knows about you?**

- If your life were trying to prove something about you, what would it be?

b. Your Negative Self-image: Who You Are Afraid You Are

If someone calls you a name that you don't identify with (for example, "You dirty, green-skinned Martian!"), there is rarely an emotional charge attached. If something upsets us, it's usually because at some level we believe it might be true. When I ask these questions in my trainings, people often react by totally denying that the negative traits they are identifying have anything to do with them. When they've had a chance to think about it, they often come back with a shocked recognition that this is in fact exactly what they've feared has been true all along.

One fact will make it easier for you to take an honest look at yourself:

Any "negative" traits you identify are not really yours—they belong to your negative self-image and were programmed into you when you were a child. By identifying them honestly, you are about to let them go!

It can be hard to look directly at your own worst fears about who and what you are—after all, you've probably spent a large portion of your life avoiding doing just that. For that reason, most of these questions point to things that reveal your negative self-image rather than your negative self-image itself:

- **What's the opposite of each of the traits of your pretend self?**

- **Which of your secrets will only be discovered after you die?**

- **Who is your least favorite person and why?**
(*Most perception is projection—we most dislike in others what we fear can be found in ourselves!*)

c. Your Authentic Self: Who You Truly Are

By identifying the traits and characteristics of your three selves, you are freeing yourself up to live more and more from the heart of who you really are—your powerful, loving, unstoppable, authentic self.

Here's a guideline to know whether you are iden-

tifying a trait or characteristic of your authentic self
or if you are caught up in the trap of your negative
self-image:

- **Who you really are always feels like coming home.**

- **Who are you when nobody's watching?**

- **If you felt totally safe, what would you do differently?**

- **Who would you be if you lived beyond fear?**

Reprogramming Your Self-image

In my experience, traditional positive thinking is
not very effective. Standing in front of the mirror
saying "Day by day in every way I am getting better
and better" doesn't really work unless you are able
to actually create a feeling of getting better at the
same time.

For example, if you were to stop reading for a
moment and tell your heartbeat to speed up, it
probably wouldn't work. But if you vividly imagine
walking down a dark alley late at night, hearing foot-
steps behind you getting closer and closer, chances
are your heartbeat will quicken.

This is because:

The key programs of human behavior are habit and imagination, and they are far more powerful than logic and willpower will ever be.

The fact is that your body responds far more readily to the vivid use of imagination than to a simple command.

That's why the way we see ourselves in our imagination is crucial to the way we live our lives.

In the early 1970s a plastic surgeon named Maxwell Maltz noticed that altering the physical appearance of his patients through surgery often created a remarkable increase in confidence and sometimes even a complete change in personality. However, some of his patients experienced no psychological benefits, no matter how spectacular the physical changes.

Maltz concluded that cosmetic correction to the external appearance of a patient doesn't work when their internal self-image is poor, or, as he put it, when they were "scarred on the inside."

So he taught those clients a simple visualization technique that created a dramatic change in their self-image. To his delight and surprise, it did as much—or more—for his patients as the actual surgery.

SMALL CHANGE, BIG RESULTS

One of the most profound examples of how a small change can quickly and easily reprogram our self-image was demonstrated in a study by social psychologist Steven J. Sherman. He set out to see if he could increase the number of volunteers in a given area that would go door-to-door collecting for the American Cancer Society.

He contacted a number of residents in the area by phone, explaining that he was doing a survey, and he asked them to predict what they would say if asked to go door to door for three hours collecting for a very good cause. Because no one wanted to see themselves as uncharitable, nearly all of them said they would volunteer.

A few days later, a representative from the American Cancer Society called the same people. The result of them committing themselves during the survey?

A phenomenal 700 percent increase in volunteers!

By teaching his patients who had a negative self-image to repeatedly imagine themselves as they ideally wanted to be, he noticed they became happier and more at peace with themselves in a matter of days.

There is a story that when Michelangelo was asked how he carved such beautiful angels, he replied, "I see the angel in the stone, and I chip away at everything around it."

Reprogramming your self-image is a lot like that—less a function of trying to be more like who you wish you were and more of recognizing the magnificence of who you really are.

Remember, our possibilities at any moment in life are computed not from how we like to think of ourselves but from whom we truly believe we are. So the more you align your self-image with the reality of your authentic self, the richer and more rewarding your life will be. This is not a new concept and is contained in every spiritual system of teaching on the planet.

Opposite is a variation on Dr. Maltz's original visualization, updated to incorporate the latest findings in brain science and self-image psychology. When I guide my clients and the participants in my trainings through it, they often report life-changing insights and find themselves unable to view themselves or the world in the same way afterward.

By repeating this simple exercise at least once a day every day for a week, you will allow your self-image to easily integrate with your authentic self. . . .

REPROGRAMMING YOUR SELF-IMAGE FOR SUCCESS

1. Take a few moments to relax and breathe deeply. As your muscles relax, it becomes easier and easier to unleash your imagination.

2. Now, imagine another you standing in front of you. This is the most magnificent you that you can imagine—your authentic self.

3. Take a moment to feel totally happy with your authentic self. Look at the way that the authentic you stands, breathes, smiles, walks, and talks. Look at how the authentic you speaks to others. Notice how the authentic you handles problems and goes for goals.

4. Now, step into and synthesize with your authentic self. See through the eyes of your authentic self, hear through the ears of your authentic self, and feel how it feels so good to live life as your authentic self!

5. Finish your programming session by taking a minute to daydream about how your life will be different as you live more and more from your authentic self. You can imagine yourself living authentically in any number of real situations from your past, present, and future.

> "Our deepest fear is not that we are inadequate, Our deepest fear is that we are powerful beyond measure. It's our light, not our darkness, that most frightens us. We ask ourselves: who am I to be brilliant, gorgeous, talented, and fabulous? Actually, who are you not to be? You are a child of the universe. Your playing small doesn't serve the world. There is nothing enlightening about shrinking, so that other people won't feel insecure around you. We are born to make manifest the glory of the universe that is within us. It's not just in some of us: it is in everyone. And as we let our own light shine, we unconsciously give other people permission to do the same. And as we are liberated from our own fear, our presence automatically liberates others."
>
> MARIANNE WILLIAMSON

Some Closing Thoughts

As you begin to live the truth of your authentic self, it will become easier and easier to act consistently with that truth. This snowball effect (the larger it gets, the faster it goes, the larger it gets, etc.)—what philosopher R. Buckminster Fuller called "precession"— is what will allow you to make dramatic changes in only seven days.

Once we make a commitment, the rest of us aligns with it. Rather than attach yet another image or limited personality onto your definition of "self," the work you have done today will allow your greater possibilities and potential to come through. I personally believe that if there is a reason or purpose to life, this may well be a key part of it.

All truly successful people accept their brilliance—they are not embarrassed by it. While aligning your self-image with the reality of your authentic self is not the answer to all of life's problems, it will help you to respond to your life more resourcefully. As who you think you are and who you really are become more and more aligned, you will begin to feel truly good about yourself, even before your life changes on the outside.

And as I've found out for myself, the better you feel on the inside, the better your life will become.

I want you to know you are unique—there is no one who has ever lived who can do things *exactly* the way you do them. You have a special gift of uniqueness to bring to the world—over the next six days, we'll identify that gift and begin to work on ways you can share it with the world!

Until tomorrow,

Paul McKenna

P.S. Would you like to be able to feel just about whatever you want whenever you want to feel it?

Tomorrow, I'm going to share with you the secrets of how to master your emotions and run your own brain, and you're going to learn how your state of mind and body, your emotions, affects everything in your life. . . .

DAY TWO

A User's Manual for Your Brain

Master your emotions and
release your full potential

BEFORE YOU BEGIN TODAY:

- Listen to the mind-programming session on the CD
- Take a few moments to go through the Reprogramming Your Self-image for Success exercise from Day One:

1. Relax and breathe deeply. As your muscles relax, it becomes easier and easier to unleash your imagination.

2. Now, imagine another you standing in front of you. This is the most magnificent you that you can imagine—your authentic self.

3. Take a moment to feel totally happy with your authentic self. Look at the way that the authentic you stands, breathes, smiles, walks, and talks. Look at how the authentic you speaks with others. Notice how the authentic you handles problems and goes for goals.

4. Now, step into and synthesize with your authentic self. See through the eyes of your authentic self, hear through the ears of your authentic self, and feel how it feels so good to live life as your authentic self!

Finish your programming session by taking a minute to daydream about how your life will be different as you live more and more from your authentic self. You can imagine yourself living authentically in any number of real situations from your past, present, and future.

TWO MONKS WERE WANDERING through the forest when they came upon a beautiful courtesan standing on the banks of a flooded stream. Because they had sworn a vow of chastity, the younger monk ignored the woman and crossed the stream quickly.

Realizing that the beautiful woman could not safely cross the stream by herself, the older monk gathered her up in his arms and carried her across the stream. Once they had reached the other side, he gently returned her to the ground. She smiled her thanks, and the two monks continued on their way.

The young monk quietly seethed as he replayed the incident again and again in his own mind.

"How could he?" the young monk thought angrily to himself. "Does our vow of chastity mean nothing to him?" The more the young monk thought about what he had seen, the angrier he became, and the argument in his head grew louder: "Why, had I done such a thing I would've been thrown out of our order. This is disgusting. I may not have been a monk as long as he has, but I know right from wrong."

He looked over at the older monk to see if he at least was showing remorse for what he had done, but the man seemed as serene and peaceful as ever.

Finally, the young monk could stand it no longer.

"How could you do that?" he demanded. "How could you even look at that woman, let alone pick her up and carry her? Do you not remember your vow of chastity?"

The older monk looked surprised, then smiled with great kindness in his eyes.

"I am no longer carrying her, brother. Are you?"

The 1000-Yard Walk

Have you ever wondered how some athletes or stage performers suddenly seem to come alive when it is their time to perform?

When Elvis Presley arrived at a new concert venue, he would have his dressing-room trailer placed exactly 1000 yards away from the arena. No matter what state of mind he was in when he left his dressing room, he would use the 1000-yard walk to guide himself into a state of confidence and charisma that was so tangible people would sense his presence and begin cheering even before he entered the building.

Today, I am going to share with you the secrets of mastering your emotions, and guide you through a series of exercises that will enable you to bring your most confident, charismatic self to any endeavor. You will learn the basic building blocks of any emotional state, and practice feeling the way you want to feel in an instant. Before we're done, I'll even share with you the technique that helped me turn my life around when I was first setting out on the path of self-mastery.

But in order to master our emotions, we must first begin by understanding what they are and how they operate. . . .

What Is an Emotional State?

Have you ever witnessed the same event as someone else and found out later that they had a completely different experience of it from you? How is it possible that you could both be in the same place at the same time and yet experience things so differently?

Or take the example of heights—some people won't even climb a ladder, while others delight in climbing tall mountains or throwing themselves out of airplanes from 30,000 feet above the earth.

The difference in both cases arises from the emotional states you are in at the time. Love, anger, confidence, fear, apathy, and curiosity are all emotional states. We are constantly going into and out of these different states of being all day long, and each of them is as individual and unique to us as our own fingerprint.

An emotional state can be defined as "the sum total of all the neurological processes occurring within somebody at any one time." A simpler way of thinking about it is that an emotional state is the mood you are in at any given moment.

We've all experienced many unresourceful states, such as depression, anger, and fear. Similarly, we've all had times where we felt filled with resourceful states such as confidence, optimism, joy, and determination.

This is important because:

All human behavior is the result of state.

INTERNAL REPRESENTATIONS
The pictures and sounds we make
in our mind and how we make them

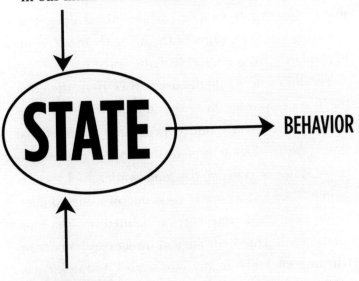

PHYSIOLOGY
Posture, muscular
tension, breathing, etc

Anything excellent that you have ever done or witnessed anyone else do is the result of the emotional state you or they were in at the time.

Today, you'll learn how to program your mind to experience more of the states you want in more of the situations you want to experience them!

Where Do Feelings Come From?

At first glance, it appears that how we feel in any moment is the result of events outside of us. Something happens in the world and we react to it by changing emotional states automatically. For example, imagine someone you are extremely attracted to. Now imagine that person has just walked into the room behind you. If you're like most people, your state just changed!

In fact, most of us are completely unaware of how we are making our feelings from moment to moment. In reality, there is an internal process that takes place in the gap between the event and your reaction to it.

Physiology

One way in which we are constantly affecting our state is through the way we use our body. Changes in our posture, breathing, muscle tension, and facial expression all affect our feelings and behavior. If you use your body differently, you will have a completely different experience of being alive.

For example, take a few moments now to think of a time when you felt particularly nervous—perhaps before standing up to give a presentation at work, or before asking a particularly difficult question of someone you really care about.

STOP!

Wherever you are, plant your feet firmly on the floor, put your shoulders back, put a big silly grin on your face, and take a deep breath. Now try to think of that unpleasant situation without changing your posture. Keep your shoulders back, your feet flat, and your teeth shining!

If you've done what I just asked, you've probably already noticed that either your feelings about the situation have changed or you're no longer able to think about it in the same way.

Our muscular tension or relaxation, breathing, and body posture all influence our states. If your body is tense it is producing different chemicals to when it is relaxed, so of course you will feel different and think different thoughts.

Internal Representations

The other key determining factor in how we feel from moment to moment is the pictures we make in our imagination and the way we talk to ourselves in our head. We refer to these images and sounds as internal representations, and they are just that—representations of reality, not reality itself.

Your internal representations of reality are unique to you—your own personal way of per-

> "We don't see things as they are, but rather as we are."
>
> ANAÏS NIN

ceiving the world. They are your own map of the world, but as with any map, they are incomplete and filled with generalizations, deletions, and distortions.

This is the reason why two people can witness the exact same event and yet experience it completely differently. In the words of the father of modern linguistics, Count Alfred Korzybski, "the map is not the territory."

The Movies of Your Mind

In my experience, *everybody* has the ability to visualize. To prove this to yourself, answer the following questions:

1. What does your front door look like? What color is it? Which side is the handle on?

2. What was the first car you ever drove? What did it look like? What color was it?

In order to answer any of these questions, you had to go into your imagination and make pictures. Now, for 99 percent of people, these images will not be "photo quality"—and that's a good thing. If your internal images were as realistic as what you see in the real world, you wouldn't be able to tell the difference!

Similarly, we all have the ability to talk to ourselves and make sounds in our mind. Sometimes, this ability can uplift us. For example, think of a song you like or your favorite piece of music. Remember the sound of the ocean, or hear the voice of someone you love offering you some honest praise.

On the other hand, have you ever had an argument with someone and even hours later you keep replaying all the nasty things they said to you that make you feel bad?

Let's do an experiment. . . .

Imagine you have been asked to go to a party. Imagine standing awkwardly in the kitchen. There is nobody around you that you know. Your least favorite music is playing much too loudly in the background.

On a scale from 1 to 10, how much do you want to go to the party?

Now, imagine standing confidently and comfortably, surrounded by lots of fun people who are really interested in spending time with you. In the background, you hear your favorite piece of music come on at just the right volume.

On a scale from 1 to 10, how appealing is the party now?

If you experienced any difference at all between those two scenarios, you can recognize how the quality of your internal representations will largely determine the quality of your life. Yet too many people exert more control over the movies they go to on the outside than the movies they play in their mind. That's an example of your brain running you instead of you running your brain.

Recently I worked with a rock star who had a fear of flying. When we stepped back and took a look at the sequence of pictures and sounds that he made in his mind, it was easy to understand how he could create such intense fear in just a few seconds.

As soon as he even thought about going to the airport he'd make a great big picture of the check-in desk and say to himself, "This is going to be bad!" Then he would imagine boarding the plane. As the door closed, he'd say to himself, "I can't get out!" He'd imagine the plane taking off and the cabin filling with smoke, everyone screaming as it crashed to the ground in a ball of flames, and then his little daughter sitting at home saying, "Where's Daddy?"

Now, I don't know about you, but watching that mental horror movie even once is enough to make anyone scared, and he was playing it over and over again in his mind. Each time he watched it, he felt worse, and the worse he felt, the more horrific he made the movie!

Now, not only do I not have a fear of flying, I actually enjoy flying.

When I know I am taking a flight, I think about where I am going and who I will see. I say to myself, "This is going to be good!" in an excited voice. Then

I imagine myself sitting back and relaxing, no telephone ringing, a nice meal, a fun movie, and, of course, flight attendants!

Once the rock star learned to change the movies in his mind, he began to feel better about flying. Soon, he had reconditioned himself to the point where he was actually looking forward to his next tour. The moral of the story is this:

As you learn to change the pictures and sounds in your mind, you too will get conscious control of your life.

Let's try another experiment.

Think of someone who annoys you, or whom you find it stressful to think about or spend time with—remember their face. Now as you look at their face in your imagination, ask yourself:

- **Is it a color image or is it black and white?**

- **Are you making it to the left, to the right, or right in front of you?**

- **Is it big or small?**

- **Light or dark?**

- **Moving or still?**

Now let's play with the way you are currently representing that person in your mind. Try out each of these changes in turn and notice what happens:

MOVIES OF YOUR MIND

1. If your representation of that person is moving, freeze-frame the picture so it is still.
2. If the image has any color in it, drain it all away until it looks like an old black-and-white photograph.
3. Shrink the image until it's tiny.
4. Move the location of the image so it's farther away.
5. Give the person a clown's nose, pink hair, and Mickey Mouse ears.
6. Imagine the sound of their voice. Then alter it by giving them a deep, sexy voice. Change it again until they sound like a squeaky little mouse.

By making these changes in your internal representations, you are reprogramming the way you feel. Think of the person again in that new way . . . now how do you feel about them? It's very likely they no longer trigger the stressful response. Not only do you almost certainly feel differently now, but next time you meet this person you'll feel differently, which means they'll respond differently to you, changing the dynamic of your relationship for the better.

The general principle that we are working with is this:

Images that are bigger, brighter, and bolder have greater emotional intensity than those that are duller, dimmer, and farther away.

Next, let's find out what an amazing difference it makes to be inside and outside of a memory. Here's another technique for running your brain, called "dissociation":

1. **Think of a mildly stressful or uncomfortable memory.**

2. **As you notice what image or images come to mind, step out of yourself so you can see the back of your head. Pull back from that image and mentally move as far away from the image as you can. Step all the way out of the picture so you can see yourself way over there, still in it. This process of disassociating reduces the intensity of the feelings the image was creating.**

Now, let's do it the other way around and step into a positive picture. This is called "association":

1. **Think of a time in your life when you felt great, and once again allow an image to come to mind.**

2. **This time, step into that image so you're seeing through your own eyes, hearing through your ears, and feeling great in your body.**

3. **Make the image bigger, the sounds louder, and the feelings stronger.**

It's easy—to reduce the intensity, step out and move back; to increase the intensity, step in and make it bigger.

Recently I was at a dinner party and sat next to a lady who was telling me how she was having trouble sleeping since she had been involved in a motorcycle accident. When I asked her to remember what was making her feel so bad, she described the horror of the crash scene as if it was happening to her all over again. Clearly, she was remembering what happened from *inside* the picture (associated).

I asked her to simply step out of the memory (dissociate) until she could see the back of her head as she floated the picture far into the distance and made it black and white. Instantly, the tension in her face reduced as her muscles softened. I told her that if she ever thought about the incident in future, she should only ever do it dissociated. Two weeks later she called me to say that she had been sleeping beautifully and was feeling much better in herself. Here's a simple chart you can use for reference:

To diminish unpleasant or stressful experiences:	To intensify positive or resourceful experiences:
• Step out of the image (dissociate)	• Step fully into the image (associate)
• Make the image still	• Make the image into a movie
• Make the image smaller and farther away	• Make the image larger and closer
• Make the image black and white, dull, or out of focus	• Intensify the colors, increase the brightness and clarity
And	And
• Make the sounds farther away, smaller, and quieter	• Make the sounds closer, larger, and louder (unless it is an experience of peace and quiet)

The power of internal representations can even turn a loser into a winner. A number of years ago an Olympic champion who was experiencing a loss of confidence came to me. His sports psychologist had told him to visualize winning the race as often as he could throughout the day.

Although he had imagined winning his race hundreds of times, he didn't feel any more confident. In fact, he was now really worried about two other competitors. When I asked him *how* he imagined winning, it turned out that he was dissociated from the experience, standing outside of the picture. Essentially, he was telling his brain that the winning was for someone else.

But when I asked him to think about the competitors who worried him, it turned out he was making big, bright pictures of them looking confident and strong. I simply told him to step in (associate) to the picture of winning while taking the pictures of his competitors and shrinking them down into tiny black-and-white images. He practiced a few times until he could do it automatically. The next day he went out and beat his personal best in practice.

In a nutshell:

The way you feel from moment to moment is a direct result of the way you are using your body and the pictures and sounds you are making in your mind.

Now that you know how to influence your state, you don't have to be at the mercy of others or of circumstances to make you feel a particular way. By taking responsibility for the pictures in your mind, the things you say to yourself (and how you say them), and the way you use your body, you can now begin to choose how you want to feel in any situation.

The Inner Critic

Nothing takes the wind out of your sails more quickly than a few critical comments made by the wrong person at the wrong time. And the worst critic you

> *"That voice inside your head is not the voice of God. It just sounds like it thinks it is."*
> CHERI HUBER

will ever encounter is the one who lives inside your own mind. The way you talk to yourself has a profound impact on your emotional state.

For example, when you make a mistake, consider the tone of voice you use when you talk to yourself.

Do you say, "Oh, goody, another learning experience!" or is it something more like, "You stupid idiot,
you really screwed up this time!" or "When are you
ever going to learn?"

Remember a time when you made a big mistake
and recall how you spoke to yourself. What does
it sound like? Is it critical, is it angry, sarcastic, or
resigned?

Many people presume that just because there's a
voice inside their head they have to listen to it. But
criticism is meant to be constructive, and if what
your inner voice says is not supporting you, try this
simple experiment. . . .

THE INNER CRITIC

1. Stop for a moment and talk to yourself in your critical voice, saying all those nasty things in that unpleasant tone.

2. Now, notice where you make that voice. Does it seem to be coming from inside your head or outside? Is it at the front, the sides, or the back?

3. Extend your arm and stick out your thumb.

4. Wherever the critical voice was, move it down your arm to the tip of your thumb, so it's now speaking to you from there.

5. Next, slow it down and change the tone of it. Make it sound sexy, or speed it up so it sounds like Mickey Mouse.

It sounds much less threatening like that, doesn't it?

Now, even though it's easy to change the voice in your mind, it's very important to remember that the intention of the critical voice is positive—to stop you from making mistakes and to help you do things better. However, criticism needs to be constructive if it's going to be of any use.

Imagine that you wanted to help a child to learn something new. If you were continually yelling at them about how useless they were every time they made a mistake, they would quickly lose confidence. However, if you use an encouraging tone of voice while pointing out what to watch out for or maybe a better way to do things, you will create an entirely different result.

Try this approach now with yourself:

1. **Remember a time when you made a mistake and you harshly criticized yourself. Recall exactly what you said.**

2. **Now ask yourself, "How could I say the same message in an encouraging way?"**

3. **Step back into yourself at that time you made the mistake. This time, give yourself the constructive criticism instead.**

Over the next few days, pay particular attention to how you talk to yourself. Play with your tone of the voice and the content of the message until you feel better in yourself.

The point is this:

You have a choice. You are in control.

How to Feel What You Want, When You Want

While it is a wonderful thing to be able to change your state in the moment, it is even more useful to be able to consistently feel resourceful in those situations that demand your best. Top Olympic athletes don't train for four years physically and then "hope" they'll feel good on the day. They program their minds and bodies to "automatically" go into great states when it matters most, in the moment of competition.

For the purpose of giving you an experience of programming your body and mind for success, I am going to take you through two simple exercises in boosting your self-confidence in any situation. You can return to this section at any time and substitute whatever feeling you want.

The more you practice these exercises, the more certain it is that you will become confident at a rate that is comfortable to you.

Whether you experience this boost in confidence straight away or whether it happens a bit more each time you practice doesn't matter. For example, I've seen people who have been shaking with nerves easily overcome their fear in just a few minutes; I've also seen people who were paralyzed by stage fright gradually evolve to the point where they can talk to an audience like they've been doing it all their lives.

Let's get started. Read through the whole technique first so you're familiar with each step, then go for it!

INSTANT CONFIDENCE BOOSTER

1. Hold your head high in a comfortable and relaxed position on your shoulders. Let your spine support you. Imagine that a golden thread runs vertically up through your spine and straight up to the sky and that that thread supports you. Let yourself relax, safely held by that thread. This relaxed upright stance is the natural position of confidence and it will soon be as natural to you as breathing.

2. Now, remember a time when you felt totally confident. Return fully to that time now, seeing what you saw, hearing what you heard, and feeling how good you felt. (If you can't remember a specific time, just imagine how much better your life would be if you were totally confident and secure—if you had all the power, strength, and self-belief you could ever need.)

3. Now, make the colors brighter and richer, the sounds louder, and allow your feelings of confidence to intensify.

4. Notice where that feeling of confidence is strongest in your body. Give this feeling of confidence a color, and move that color up to the top of your head and down to the tip of your toes. Double the brightness. Double it again!

5. Repeat steps 2–4 at least five more times. Vividly imagine that event where you are confident again in detail. You can use the same experience or add in new ones each time.

The Confidence Switch

Now that you know how to boost your confidence whenever you choose, how would you like to be able to have a "switch" that allows you to fire off that confident feeling whenever you need it?

In the late 1900s a Russian scientist called Pavlov conducted some famous experiments where he would offer food to his dog and at the same time ring a bell. After he had done this several times the dog associated the bell with food, and within a short while he would only have to ring the bell and the dog would salivate. He had created an association between a bell and feeding time. There was no logical connection between the two things, but through constant repetition, a neurological connection was created in the mind of the dog.

The simple scientific reason is this: the brain is a mass of millions of neural pathways, with each idea or memory moving along its own path. Whenever we do something new, we create a new neural pathway so we can re-access that experience again more easily. Each time we repeat a particular behavior, we strengthen the associated neural pathway, just as when you walk down a path through a field it becomes a clearer path.

Research has shown that these neural pathways in the brain actually get physically larger through repetition of behavior. That is how people become "hardwired" to certain automatic behaviors, such as smoking and overeating. We can use that same mental architecture to design pathways to success and happiness, and to create associations that allow us to "switch on" certain feelings whenever we want them.

I remember years ago when I teamed up with a huge promoter who booked my live hypnosis show into the biggest theater in London. I'd never played any place like it before, and when I first stood on the stage a few days before the show and looked out at the massive empty auditorium I started to feel fear in my stomach.

In order to "switch on" the level of confidence I knew I needed to perform at my best, I did the same exercise that you're about to do. I created an association between a feeling of confidence and a simple physical gesture, and I vividly imagined the event going beautifully.

The night of the performance I was feeling a bit unsure about how I would feel once I was out there. However, the moment I walked out on the stage it was as though a sheet of calm came over me and I glided through a perfect performance. Despite the inevitable challenges that came my way, I felt so calm and in control that I handled all of them effortlessly.

I'm going to guide you through accessing a strong positive state. Each time you experience a peak of the good feeling, press the thumb and middle finger of either hand together to create an association between confidence and the physical gesture. Over time, this gesture will become your confidence "switch," enabling you to access your most confident states at will.

Here's the process, exactly as I use it for myself. Once again, before you undertake this technique read through it first so you know each step. . . .

THE CONFIDENCE SWITCH

1. Remember a time when you felt really, really confident. Fully return to it now—see what you saw, hear what you heard, and feel how good you felt. (If you can't remember a time, imagine how much better your life would be if you were totally confident—if you had all the power, strength, and self-belief you could ever need!)

2. As you keep going through this memory, make the colors brighter and richer, the sounds louder, and the feelings stronger.

3. As you feel these good feelings, squeeze the thumb and middle finger of either hand together.

4. Now, squeeze the thumb and finger together and relive that good feeling.

5. Repeat steps 1–4 several times with different positive memories until just squeezing your thumb and finger together begins to bring back those good feelings.

6. Still holding your thumb and finger together, think about a situation in which you want to feel more confident. Imagine things going perfectly, going exactly the way you want them to go. See what you'll see, hear what you'll hear, and feel how good it feels.

Practice this every day. The mind is very sensitive, and as you feel more confident running through those scenarios in your imagination, you will feel more confident when they occur in the real world.

Whenever you feel challenged, simply turn on your confidence switch by squeezing your thumb and middle finger together, concentrate for a few moments, and access your inner state of confidence!

The Secret of Charisma

We all know people who have a kind of magic quality about them. When they walk into a room, it lights up and we feel drawn to them. They don't have to be the life and soul of the party, but something about them makes them mysteriously attractive. Many Hollywood stars are not brilliant actors, but something seems to emanate from inside them that appeals to many, many people. That is the quality we call charisma.

Charismatic people feel comfortable in themselves. Because they are content with who they are, they aren't desperately looking for the approval of others and they aren't trying to manipulate others into liking them. Ironically, that's why we feel drawn to them.

I'm now going to guide you through two of my favorite techniques for cranking up your self-appreciation, making you feel more at peace with yourself and more charismatic to the world.

THE EYES OF LOVE

1. If it's appropriate, close your eyes and think of someone who loves or deeply appreciates you. Remember how they look, and imagine they are standing in front of you now.

2. Gently step out of your body and into the body of the person who loves you. See through their eyes, hear through their ears, and feel the love and good feelings they have as you look at yourself. Really notice in detail what it is that they love and appreciate about you. Recognize and acknowledge those amazing qualities that perhaps you hadn't appreciated about yourself until now.

3. Step back into your own body and take a few moments to enjoy those good feelings of knowing that you are loved and appreciated exactly as you are.

This next technique is excellent for making you feel much more attractive as a person and was devised by my colleague Michael Breen. In order to do it you will need a mirror. You are going to create an association between your reflection and the many compliments you have received throughout your lifetime.

One of the reasons this technique works so well is because everyone receives compliments and praise from time to time. Sometimes it may seem trivial, like, "Hey, you're looking good today!" or "My friend thinks you're gorgeous!" At other times, it may be more significant, like, "Do you know how much people respect you?" or "Thank you for being who you are and doing what you do."

Sincere, positive appreciation from others, especially appreciation that you might not have been able to see or fully perceive from the point of view you had at the time, can be valuable in learning to appreciate your own qualities more fully and enhance your self-respect now.

WHAT'S RIGHT WITH YOU

1. Standing in front of a mirror with your eyes closed, recall a specific time when you were paid a compliment by someone you respect or trust. Run through the experience in vivid detail.

2. As you recall the compliment, and the sincerity of the person who said it, pay particular attention to your feelings of trust and regard for the other person.

3. When you feel that as strongly as possible, open your eyes and look in the mirror. Allow yourself to really see what that person saw and notice how that feels.

4. When you are really feeling wonderful in yourself, squeeze together your thumb and middle finger. Allow the feelings of self-love and self-respect to blend with the feelings of confidence that are already there.

Remember to use these techniques every day and don't be too surprised at how confident and charismatic you become. As your confidence increases each day, you'll find yourself naturally doing things that you used to only dream of!

Developing Your Emotional Intelligence

OK, we're coming to the end of one of the most important lessons you will ever learn. We have seen how we can change our feelings by modifying the way we use our body, the way we talk to ourselves and the pictures we make in our mind. So does this mean we'll never feel angry, sad, or fearful again?

Well, sometimes, for some people, it might be that simple, but for most of us there's another aspect of our emotional life that has to be considered.

Working with your feelings is really learning to use your emotional intelligence to the full. There is a whole world of understanding and insight available through your emotions.

An emotion is a bit like someone knocking on your door to deliver a message. If the message is urgent, it knocks loudly. If it is very urgent, it knocks very loudly. If you don't answer the door, it knocks louder and louder and louder until you open the door. Then it delivers its message. As soon as you understand even part of it, it becomes part of your self-understanding. You are changed, and the emotion has done its job.

This does not mean that all emotions are immediately infallible guides to action. Far from it. But to reach the wisdom of our emotions, we must work with them. We have to remember that we experience a huge range of feelings—almost as great a range as we have thoughts. Some of our thoughts are banal and meaningless; others are meaningful and worthwhile. It is the same with our feelings. Some are trivial; others are profound.

Unfortunately, for the last three hundred years western culture has woefully undervalued the emotions. Indeed, most western cultures place a high value on suppressing and ignoring emotional reactions. Yet learning to handle our emotions and to understand them is a fundamental part of growing up, just like learning to use our mind to think clearly, or using our hands to write or draw or make things.

At this point, you may be wondering: How can I tell the difference between emotions that are just reactions to the pictures in my head and emotions that have an important message I need to learn from?

The answer is simple. If an emotion is unimportant, or no longer truly relevant to your life, it vanishes when you change the pictures in your head. If it is important and relates to a real, current situation that you need to learn from, it will come back, again and again and again. In that case, when the emotion turns up you need to listen and learn from it. As for how to do that, read on. . . .

The Negativity Fast

The final technique for today is one of the most powerful in the whole book, and everyone can benefit from it. I first began using it in 1990, and I almost immediately noticed a remarkable upturn in my confidence and ability to solve problems and reach my goals.

We have already seen that the more often we repeat a pattern of behavior, the stronger that pattern becomes. When we indulge in negativity over the years, we literally hardwire ourselves to be negative.

For the rest of the week, you are going to interrupt that pattern. You are going to starve yourself of negativity and retrain yourself to be more positive instead. Don't just read this, LIVE IT FOR THE NEXT WEEK. This process alone will rewrite the operating software of your mind—it's a process that will serve you well for the rest of your life!

Here's how it works:

For the next week, whenever you feel bad about anything, stop what you're doing (as soon as it is safe to do so) and follow these five easy steps. . . .

THE NEGATIVITY FAST

1. **Ask yourself what you are feeling bad about and notice what image, sound, or words come to mind.**

   Remember, your emotions are like signals, letting you know when you need to pay extra attention to some aspect of your experience. Every feeling in your body is linked to an internal picture, sound, or the words you say to yourself in your mind.

2. **Listen for the message or positive intention of the emotion.**

   Negative emotions are just messengers sent by your mind and body to let you know it's time to pay attention to something. For example, if I have a worrying feeling and I stop and notice, what comes to mind is the image of an upcoming meeting. My mind is trying to alert me to things that might go wrong in that meeting and make sure I am well prepared.

3. **Act on the message!**

   So, in our example, I might make a list of all the things I can do to stop those problems occurring, and take action on at least one of them.

4. **Turn off the messenger.**

   This is like hanging up the phone or resetting the smoke alarm. When I've heeded my mind's warning, I drain all the color out of the image, shrink it down to the size of a postage stamp and send it off into the distance. If the picture pops

The Negativity Fast *continued*

back, it's because there's still something you
need to be aware of, so find out what it is.

5. Program your desired future.
Finally, imagine events going exactly the way you
want them to. In the example of my upcoming
meeting, I make a big, bright movie of the
meeting going perfectly and watch it all the way
up to the happy ending.

Test this amazing process out now for yourself . . .

1. **Think about something that makes you feel
    bad, and notice what image comes to mind. As
    you pay attention to that image, notice:**

    - **Is it color or black and white?**

    - **Where is it located? Is it in front of you? Or
      to the left or right?**

    - **Is it big or small?**

    - **Is it a movie, or is it a still image?**

    - **Is it a solid image, or transparent?**

    - **Is there any sound with this image?**

2. **Now STOP! All of this information is what**

gives the bad feeling its power, and you were unconscious of it going on until a moment ago. So now you are aware of it, we're going to ask what its intention is. What message does the emotion want to give you?

3. Now, take a few moments to brainstorm some ways you can solve those problems. If you have time, you can write down some notes. If not, just ask your unconscious mind to remind you at the next available opportunity.

4. Then, drain all the color out of the image, shrink it, and move it off into the distance. If it happens to reappear, ask yourself if there's anything you've missed, then just drain the color out again, shrink it so it's small, and move it far away once again.

5. Finally, take a few moments to imagine your life as you would ideally like it to be. How do you want to be? What kinds of things would you like to do? What would you most want to have?

With every new habit we take on, there is a "tipping point"—that point at which it becomes easier to exercise than not; easier to eat healthily than to eat unhealthily; easier to think rich than to think poor.

Every time you practice, you will get benefits, but you will only get the most amazing benefits of this technique if you practice it right up to and over the tipping point. Use it every time you feel bad about anything for the next week. Through the sheer repetition of this technique, you will totally recondition yourself for success. You will become more positive, energized, and optimistic. You will start to look at life with more optimism, seeing opportunities to succeed and achieve in situations where before you saw only fear, failure, and "more of the same."

Until tomorrow,

Paul McKenna

P.S. In the next chapter, I'll be sharing with you the secrets of a positive perspective—how to turn any problem into an opportunity to learn, change, and succeed!

DAY THREE

The Power of a Positive Perspective

The Art of Reframing

BEFORE YOU BEGIN TODAY:

- Listen to the mind-programming session on the CD.
- Review the Reprogramming Your Self-image for Success exercise from page 41.
- Do the following exercise in creating a positive state

1. Remember a time when you felt really, really good. Fully return to it now—see what you saw, hear what you heard, and feel how good you felt. (If you can't remember a time, imagine how much better your life would be if you were totally confident—if you had all the power, strength, and self-belief you could ever need!)

2. As you keep going through this memory, make the colors brighter and richer, the sounds louder, and the feelings stronger.

3. As you feel these good feelings, squeeze the thumb and middle finger of either hand together.

4. Now squeeze your thumb and finger together and relive that good feeling. Think about the rest of the day ahead, feeling and imagining things going perfectly, going the way you want them to go. See what you'll see, hear what you'll hear, and feel how good it feels.

Congratulations! You have just programmed yourself to have a great day.

THERE IS AN OLD, OLD STORY about a farmer in China. One year the weather was very good and his crops grew strong and high, and all his neighbors told him how lucky he was to have such a fine crop and he replied, "Maybe." Then the day before he was going to start the harvest a herd of wild horses came running off the plains and trampled all his crops flat. His neighbors came around and said how unlucky he was to lose his fine crop. The farmer replied, "Maybe." The next day the farmer's son went out with a length of rope and caught a wild stallion and three mares, and the neighbors came around to admire the horses and told the farmer how lucky he was. The farmer said, "Maybe." In the morning the farmer's son started to break in the horses and no sooner had he mounted the stallion than it threw him, and as he fell on the ground he broke his leg. The neighbors carried him indoors and commiserated with the farmer, saying how unlucky he was that his only son was so badly injured. The farmer said, "Maybe." The next day the emperor's army came to the village on the way to fight a great battle and all the able-bodied young men were press-ganged into the army. But the farmer's son was not taken because of his broken leg. All his neighbors told the farmer how lucky he was that his son had been saved from the army, and the farmer said, "Maybe."

The Power of a Positive Perspective

A couple of years ago I met the actor Will Smith at a party. I said to him that I admire his work and that I think he is a positive inspiration to lots of people. He stopped, looked at me, thought about what I had said, and replied, "Thank you—thank you very much. But I have to say," he continued, "it's been easy for me—I'm black."

> "There's no such thing as bad weather—only the wrong clothes."
>
> BILLY CONNOLLY

When I asked him about this rather extraordinary point of view, he told me that ever since he was a boy, he has made extensive use of the power of perspective. In any situation, he looks for a truthful but highly selective way of thinking that makes him feel positive and gets him excited about making things happen.

Perhaps one of the most important concepts in this book is this:

Your experience of life is primarily affected by the perspective you view it from. Depending upon the meaning we give to situations or events, we will feel and behave differently.

Some people always manage to look at things in a positive way. They have an ability to frame any situation in a way that leaves them feeling empowered and strong. They can take a seemingly negative situation and reframe it to find the positive. For these people, the glass is always half full, no matter how empty it may look to the rest of us.

Some time ago I met the former RAF officer John Nichol, who was shot down while on a mission during the Gulf War. As a result, John was horribly tortured by his Iraqi captors. When I asked him how he managed to get through this terrifying ordeal, he explained how he framed it in his mind. *He knew that no matter what, the torture and the pain would stop.* Either his captors would get bored, or he would pass out. Even though it was a terrible situation to be in, the power of his perspective of knowing it would stop was what gave him the strength to make it through.

You can change your life with the power of positive perspectives—today's lesson will teach you how.

Media and Meaning

A highly effective communicator can reframe anything to create a different perspective or interpretation. In fact, there is so much "spin" in the media today that about the only thing you can know for sure is that if you don't take responsibility for the frames you make in your life then someone else will!

> "We're not retreating, we're just advancing in another direction."
>
> GEN. GEORGE S. PATTON

- Advertisers get paid a lot of money to frame their products in the best possible light. They do it by creating the idea that somehow what they are selling will make you sexier, healthier, happier, or more stylish.

- Public relations is about arranging the truth to put across your point in the best possible light.

- Marketers, politicians, and even religions have all become expert at placing their products, services, or view of how we should lead our lives in contexts that make them appear sophisticated, worthy, or desirable.

- The news media shape our opinions of the world by which stories they choose to report. Rather than making those decisions based on what will help us make informed decisions about the world, all too often the mechanism for choosing what is featured and what gets

left out comes down to what will pull higher ratings.

In much the same way as a photographer tells you what is important in a picture by what he decides to include in the frame and what is left out, the meanings we attribute to the events in our lives are determined by the parts of our experience we choose to make important. Our interpretation of any situation depends on what we include or exclude from our frame of perception.

> "No matter how thin you slice it, there are always two sides."
> BARUCH SPINOZA

The fact is: everything is relative. When you think one situation is bad, that is because you are comparing it to something you perceive is better. One of my favorite examples of this comes in a letter from a college student to her parents:

Dear Mom and Dad,

Apologies for taking so long to write, but my writing instruments were destroyed in the fire at my apartment. I am out of the hospital and the doctor says that I should be able to lead a normal healthy life. A handsome young man named Pete saved me from the fire and kindly offered to share his apartment with me. He is very kind and polite and from a good family, so I think you'll approve when I tell you that we got married last week. I know you'll be even more excited when I tell you that you are going to be grandparents very soon.

Actually there wasn't a fire, I haven't been in the hospital, I'm not married, and I'm not pregnant, but I did fail my biology exam, and I just wanted to make sure that when I told you, you put it in a proper perspective.

Love,
Your daughter

I had a friend who demonstrated the power of comparative framing even more dramatically. For months, my friend was continually telling me how frightened he was that soon he would be forty years old and his much younger girlfriend did not want to marry him. No matter how much I attempted to reassure him, he persisted in focusing on what he considered to be "the worst thing that could happen"—that he might still be unmarried and without a family at the age of forty.

One day I noticed that he seemed calmer and was no longer complaining about his situation. When I asked him what had changed, he told me his girlfriend had recently found a lump in her breast. Though it turned out to be benign, he recognized that compared to the threat of losing her to cancer, not being married yet was little more than a minor inconvenience.

Remember, the advantage of being able to decide how you frame events is that it gives you more choices. More choices gives us greater flexibility, and as we'll see in a few moments, greater flexibility leads to an increased ability to influence the results in any situation.

Flexibility Is Power

Years ago the propellers on ships used to be attached with metal shear pins. The thinking was that by making them of the strongest materials, they would last longer and be more secure. Unfortunately, the pins were so rigid that if they hit anything, they broke. Nowadays, ship propellers are attached with flexible rubber couplings—although seemingly less

> "Whoever sets the agenda controls the outcome of the debate."
> NOAM CHOMSKY

strong than their metal counterparts, these couplings offer greater longevity and security through their flexibility.

Similarly, researchers in the relatively new science of cybernetics have found that the most powerful person in any group is invariably the most flexible. The individual who has the most ways of looking at things has the most choices, and hence the greatest possibility of controlling the outcome of any situation.

The art of reframing the world with a positive perspective is not about ignoring problems, but about having sufficient flexibility to make your point of view work for you instead of against you. When I'm working with children who have to go through an unpleasant medical procedure, I reframe it by turning it into a game; with grown-ups, I'll often help them reframe their fear as excitement and their procrastination as "perfectly timing the universe."

There's No Such Thing as "Failure"

One of the most important lessons I've learned from working with successful people over the years is that "failure" is an attitude, not an outcome. That is, it's nothing to do with the results you produce and everything to do with how you frame things.

For example, after Thomas Edison's seven hundredth unsuccessful attempt to invent the electric light, he was asked by a *New York Times* reporter, "How does it feel to have failed seven hundred times?"

The great inventor responded with a classic example of a positive perspective:

"I have not failed seven hundred times. I have not failed once. I have succeeded in proving that those seven hundred ways will not work. When I have eliminated all the ways that will not work, I will find the way that will work."

Thousands more of those successful proofs of what will not work followed, but Edison finally found "the way that will work," and in so doing, illuminated the world.

Above all, what Edison succeeded in doing was to frame his particular challenge in a way that helped keep him motivated. He was flexible enough in his thinking to give himself more choices. And you can give yourself the same flexibility!

Here's an exercise in putting the power of perspective to work in your own life:

THE FRAME GAME

1. Think about a project or goal that you made happen in the past. What frame, meaning, or perspective did you or someone else use to get and keep you motivated and involved? Examples: "My boss kept our team working hard on a project by making it about contribution to the community." "I got my son to do his homework by tying in his success at school to how much freedom I gave him around the house."

2. Think of a project or goal that you are currently working on or considering working on in the future.

3. What are some frames you could put around the project that would reduce your interest in getting involved and making it happen? Examples: "This is an experiment in failure." "Even if it works, nothing good will come of it." "This is just the latest management fad."

4 What frames could you put around the project that would increase your interest in getting involved and making it happen? Examples: "She who dies with the most friends wins." "Whatever the result, it will have been worthwhile." "The universe wants me to succeed."

A Question of Perspective

One of the most powerful framing tools we all use on a daily basis is also one of the simplest—the power of questions.

Questions determine the focus of our perception, as well as the amount of success, love, fear, anger, joy, or wonder that we experience on an ongoing basis. Some of the people I meet and work with are stuck or in pain because they are continually asking themselves negatively orientated questions.

Consider the question, "Why can't I do this?" This question assumes that a) there is something to be done and b) you can't do it.

In order to even understand the question, your mind automatically begins to search out all the reasons why "you can't do" whatever it is that you perceive needs to be done. No matter what answer you give, you are accepting the basic premise of the question.

Alternatively, imagine asking yourself, "How can I most easily make this work?" This question presupposes that a) this can work, b) there are a number of ways this can work, and c) it can be done easily. These assumptions or presuppositions act as a directional compass and your mind then searches for how to make things work.

Questions direct your focus, and you always get more of what you focus on in life. If your quality of life is poor, examine your inner questions and ask yourself how much more empowering you can make them.

Some examples of common, but unhelpful, questions are:

- **Why does this always happen to me?**

- **Why don't I like myself?**

- **Why can't I ever lose weight?**

Now, ask yourself a new question:

How can I ask this in a way that points toward the positive?

So let's learn how questions can empower us. Start by asking questions that presuppose the positive, such as:

- **What is the most elegant way I can solve this problem?**

- **How many different ways of solving this problem can I come up with?**

- **How can I most easily stop doing ___?**

These questions make your brain sort for different information and put you in a different and more resourceful state. If you are not happy with the answer you are getting back, you can either change the question or keep asking until you are. Your brain will keep searching for you until a useful answer has been found.

The Work of Byron Katie

All too often human beings become entrenched in an unresourceful place through lack of emotional flexibility. By asking questions that gently force the listener to experience things differently, I have seen people become free from years of painful emotions in a matter of minutes.

Byron Katie, author of the amazing book *Loving What Is*, uses a simple but remarkably effective set of questions that help people overcome anger, resentment, and fear very quickly. She begins by asking if there is someone you are judging harshly—someone you haven't yet forgiven for whatever it is that they've done. She asks for specific information, such as:

How do you want them to change? What should or shouldn't they do? What do you need from them in order to be happy?

Once she has elicited the perspective that is causing the resentment she asks four simple questions:

1. **Is it true?**

When people first consider whether their point of view is true, the answer is often a resounding yes. However, she follows it up with a more searching question:

2. **Can you *really* know that it's true?**

For many people it comes as a surprise that they can't know for a fact that what they think is upsetting them is true. A shift has already begun to happen.

3. **How do you react when you think that thought/ tell yourself that story?**

This question gets you in touch with the negative consequences, stress, and upset of your mind-set. It quickly becomes obvious that continuing to view the world through this frame is unproductive at best and downright damaging at worst.

4. **Who would you be without that thought/story?**

In order to honestly answer this question, you have to move outside the limitations of the negative perspective you originally wrote down. Simultaneously, you begin to feel better.

At this point, most people are ready to let the burden of the upset go and embrace their new stress-free mindset. You can work with these questions any time you want to step beyond a limiting perspective.

Possibility Questions

One of the differences between geniuses like Albert Einstein and many of the other scientists of his day was that he asked smarter questions. The types of question Einstein particularly excelled at are what I call "possibility questions." These are questions that focus the mind on what is possible but may not have ever been considered before.

Think of a situation where you've been feeling a bit stuck and ask yourself the following possibility questions:

- **What would happen if this just wasn't a problem any more?**

- What would it take for everything to be all right?

- If I knew there was a simple solution, what would it be?

- What haven't I thought of yet?

- If I made an astounding breakthrough in this area, what would it be like?

Remember the golden rule:

You always get more of what you focus on in life.

So it's vitally important to acknowledge and concentrate on your successes, great and small—on what's really healthy and rewarding around you.

EMPOWERING QUESTIONS

Here is a technique you can use to put the power of a positive perspective to work in your own life, starting now. I ask myself these questions every morning; they force me to go into a positive state in order to answer them. The more specific you are, the richer the positive state you will create!

- Who or what in my life makes me feel happiest?
- Who or what in my life makes me feel most loved?
- Who or what in my life makes me feel richest?
- Who or what in my life makes me feel most passionate?
- Who or what in my life makes me feel most empowered?

As I answer each question, I build up a vivid representation of whatever it is I am thinking about, then amplify it. For example, when I am thinking about what really makes me feel happy, I make the colors brighter, the sounds louder, and the feelings stronger. By the time I've asked and answered each question, my entire outlook has changed for the better and I'm ready to take on the day!

A New Perspective on Relationships

The secret of getting on well with others is to be able to see the world through their eyes, or, as the Native Americans put it, "to walk a mile in their moccasins."

The power of perspective helped the great Indian leader Mahatma Gandhi become a legendary negotiator. Seeing from many perspectives gave him flexibility in his thinking and actions that helped him to become a powerful negotiator. Some say he even brought about the end of the British Empire because he was flexible enough to imagine seeing things from the perspective of his opponents. During the negotiations over the future of India, he would view the situation from every possible perspective, even imagining himself standing over the shoulder of his negotiation partners and sitting in their seats until he felt he almost "knew their thoughts." Because he took the time to prepare so thoroughly, it was as though he had an answer for all of their considerations and concerns before discussions started.

In my own experience, I believe that when attempting to see a situation from the viewpoint of others it is important to bear one thing in mind:

People do what they do in order to achieve some purpose or fulfill some need.

I personally prefer to believe that most people have a positive intention behind their behavior, even when they are taking a position that seems contentious or contrary to our own best interests. When I encounter a situation such as that I often ask myself: "What beneficial intention could be behind this behavior?" This helps me to approach the conflict from a much more resourceful perspective.

If you're currently experiencing a conflict in one or more of your relationships, put this simple exercise to the test:

PUTTING YOUR RELATIONSHIPS INTO PERSPECTIVE

1. Think of somebody you are having a problem with. Return to the situation where you had a conflict, or imagine that person is standing in front of you now. See what you see, hear your internal dialogue, and take note of how you feel. Now float up out of yourself and let those feelings go.

2. Next, float into the shoes of that person you don't get along with. If you like, you can even imagine putting on their head like a virtual reality helmet. Notice how the world looks from their perspective. See yourself through their eyes. What might they be saying to themselves about the situation? How does it feel to be in their shoes? Now float out of that person and let those feelings go.

3. Next, think of someone whose intelligence and wisdom you admire. It can be a friend, mentor, or even a character from history. Step into their shoes and imagine they are watching the two of you interact. How would they perceive this situation as a neutral observer? Move to a position where you can see both yourself and the person you were having the problem with. Observe what's going on with "those people over there." What are they doing? What kinds of thing are they saying to each other? What kinds

of insight do you gain inside the mind of this wise mentor? What advice do they have for you?

4. Finally, take what you've learned and step back into your own shoes. Look at that person you were having the problems with in new ways, and choose at least one thing to say or do to move toward a happy resolution.

The Power of Beliefs

The most powerful frame we can use to shape our perspective is what we choose to believe about ourselves and the world. Over the years I've often seen how one belief can mean the difference between ordinary workers and CEOs, success and failure, also-rans and world champions. Our beliefs can determine our level of intelligence, our happiness, the quality of our relationships, even our health and success.

In many ways, what we believe has a far greater influence on our life than objective truth. For example, it doesn't really matter how far you travel around the world—you won't fall off it. But for thousands of years, the commonly held belief that the

Earth was flat meant that most people didn't even attempt to travel beyond the horizon. It only took one man who was willing to see things differently to transform the experience of the planet.

Beliefs are the windows through which you view the world. If your "belief window" is covered with too much negativity—ideas such as "the world is a dangerous place" or "people can't be trusted"—you will see a dangerous world filled with untrustworthy people. If you replace the beliefs on your window with positive ones such as "the world is a friendly place" and "I can trust myself," you get to live in a friendly world where you are able to make smart choices about every aspect of your life.

The legendary psychologist Abraham Maslow told this story about the power of beliefs:

> *A patient had no regard for himself*
> *because he believed he was a corpse, and*
> *his psychiatrist spent many sessions trying*
> *to convince him that he wasn't a corpse.*
> *Finally one day the psychiatrist*
> *asked the patient if corpses bled.*
> *The patient was adamant.*
> *"Corpses don't bleed," he insisted. "All*
> *their bodily functions have stopped."*
> *The psychiatrist then persuaded the patient*

to partake in an experiment where he
would prick his hand with a needle to
see if it bled. Sure enough, as the needle
pricked his skin he began to bleed.
With a look of amazement the patient said:
"Well, I'll be darned . . . corpses do bleed!"

Your beliefs determine your decisions, how you feel about things, and ultimately the direction you go in life. They control everything about you. In the same way that a movie projector puts an image from a piece of film onto a screen, what you perceive in the world is a manifestation of the beliefs you hold in your mind.

If you are wondering what your beliefs are, then look at how you feel about your life. Do you feel in control? Do you feel empowered? Do you feel exceptional levels of happiness most of the time?

If not, this final section of today's lesson will be very important for you. . . .

The Seven Key Beliefs of High-Achievers

Over the years I have had the opportunity to work with and study many people who are widely considered geniuses in our culture. These are extraordinary individuals from the arts, business, sports, and so on. As a result of the work I have done with them, here are what I have discovered to be the seven core success perspectives of happy, healthy high-achievers.

Remember, a belief is no more than a perspective—a window through which we view the world. When you choose to view the world though the window of these positive perspectives, you create a more resourceful point of view and can begin experiencing breakthroughs in your life immediately. Don't worry about whether or not you actually think these things are true—just vividly imagine now what your life would be like if you knew that. . . .

1. You are the expert on you.
There is an old Sufi story about a man who was looking for his keys outside his home under the bright street-lamps that lit his road. Many of his neighbors joined him in his search until one finally asked, "Where did you lose your keys?" The man replied, "Inside my house."

Amazed, the neighbor asked, "Then why are you looking out here?"

The man replied, "Because there's more light out here."

The simple fact is that nobody knows you better

than you know yourself. Even if you have spent your entire life searching for answers outside yourself, once you start looking within, the perfect answers to life's questions will pop out more and more.

2. You are not broken; you do not need to be "fixed."

In the nineteenth century, the concept of people being "broken" grabbed hold of the nascent psychiatric community and became the standard for more than a hundred years. Geniuses like Richard Bandler and modern psychologists led by such innovators as Martin Seligman and Mihaly Csikszentmihalyi (Mee-hi Chik-sentmee-hi) see things differently. The emerging field of Positive Psychology is built on the premise that if we want to replicate mental health, we need to study people who are healthy, not those that are sick.

I've learned in my years of working with people in all walks of life that everyone does what they do for a very good reason, even though the reason may seem inappropriate to the outside world. Any dysfunctional behavior has a positive intent or once served a purpose that has since been outgrown.

For example, if someone has a fear of flying, it might be for any number of reasons, but if we assume the phobia has a positive intent, we know it will probably come down to the desire to be safe. As your unconscious mind finds new ways of keeping you safe without the unnecessary phobic response, the phobia itself becomes unnecessary.

This is why, using modern psychological techniques, we can now cure lifetime phobias in a matter of minutes.

3. You already have all the resources you need to succeed.

Are you confident about tying your shoelaces or shopping for groceries? Then you already have the resources of confidence within you. Therefore, you can feel confident about speaking in public or approaching a person you feel attracted to or anything else you desire.

Have you ever felt love in your heart, for a parent or child or even a pet? Then you can be more loving with your partner, family, or even yourself.

The only difference between you and someone who is already living their genius is learning how to access your resources at the appropriate times. This book helps you to do that!

4. **You can accomplish anything if you break the task down into small enough chunks.**

A few years ago a man ate an airplane over a period of a few months by breaking it down into tiny pieces. While I certainly don't recommend attempting to replicate his feat, the fact is that any skill can be learned and any problem solved if it is broken down into small enough pieces.

When you train your brain to look at huge tasks in terms of simple, achievable steps, the huge tasks become much more possible. We naturally do this already. For example, when you want to remember a phone number, you break it into smaller chunks; if you want to buy an expensive item, like a car or a house, you pay in small, manageable installments.

My point is this:

If you want to knock down the wall between you and the life of your dreams, it's best to do it one brick at a time!

5. **If what you are doing isn't working, do something else.**

In his bestselling business book *Who Moved My Cheese?*, author Spencer Johnson points out the difference between humans and rats. If rats discover what they're doing isn't working, they do something else; if humans discover what they're doing isn't working, they look for someone to blame.

I often hear people who are stuck say, "But I've always done it like that" or "I'm just not that kind of person." The truth is, what feels normal to us is more a product of our programming than our potential. If you want to begin producing different results in your life, you'll need to step outside your comfort zone and do something different.

> "Would you like me to give you a formula for success?
>   It's quite simple really. Double your rate of failure."
>
> THOMAS J. WATSON, FOUNDER OF IBM

6. **There is no such thing as failure, only feedback.**

When have you failed? When you decide to stop learning. Until then, every response you get is valuable information that can be used to tell you whether your actions are taking you closer to or further away from what you want. In the same way, when an airplane flies to its destination, it's off course 90 percent of the time, constantly adjusting its flight path to keep on course.

In fact, successful people recognize that success is what happens when you're done failing. In my experience, the people who've "made it" have one thing in common—they've made more mistakes than the people who haven't. Every mistake or failure is a learning opportunity in disguise.

"Failure" is a requisite part of the learning process, not the end of the learning process. In fact, people don't fail—strategies, tactics, and plans fail. What do you do if your strategy, tactic, or plan fails to produce the desired result? Change your strategy, tactic, or plan until you find one that succeeds!

Fear of failure is a potent demotivator, but it loses its power over us if we lessen its emotional charge. This week, choose an area of your life where you're having difficulty, and give yourself permission to "fail" at least ten times. You'll have to define failure for yourself—if you're in sales this might mean collecting at least ten rejections; if you're a writer, give yourself permission to write at least ten lousy pages.

> "I have learnt more from my failures than my successes."
> RICHARD BRANSON

Success is often made sweeter when it takes a little effort to arrive at. Once you realize that failure is not an end but rather an occasionally frustrating stepping stone, it loses its negative charge and becomes an essential companion on your journey to happiness, success, and well-being.

7. **You are creating your future NOW.**

When I am working with a private client on their goals, I will often ask, "If you carry on as you are, will you achieve it?"

To my amazement, they always know the answer, and more often than not that answer is "no."

One of the most significant differences I've noticed between the people who succeed and the ones who struggle is whether they look into the past or the present to create their future. If you continually look to the past, you will always feel that history is doomed to repeat itself; if you look to the present, you will always find there is some new choice you can make to enhance your possibilities.

No matter how much you've struggled in the past, every moment of every day provides you with an opportunity to make new choices and create new results.

THE NEW BELIEF GENERATOR

I'd like to finish today with a simple exercise for your imagination that will enable you to train your unconscious mind to operate out of a new perspective more easily.

Choose one of the seven beliefs you have just read about that you believe will make a real difference in the way you live your life . . .

1. Stop for a moment and imagine that in front of you is "another you." A "you" who already holds that belief you would like to make your own. Maybe you believe that you are confident, motivated, deserve love, are full of happy, vibrant energy.

2. Now, imagine what already having that belief enables that other you to achieve. Is that other you motivated? Confident? Strong? Successful?

3. Imagine that other you demonstrating those things effortlessly. How do they behave? How does that other you talk to themself? What kind of voice tone do they use? How do they carry themselves? How do they move?

4. If it isn't quite how you want it, make the adjustments that make you feel better. Allow your intuition to be your guide.

5. When you're satisfied with the other you, step into them. Take the new perspective and behaviors into you.

6. Now think of a situation that you would like to view from your new perspective. Think through

The New Belief Generator *continued*

what it's like to have that new perspective and what it will help you to achieve. How are things going to be so much better now?

7. For the next few weeks, act as if your new belief is true. Even if it feels like you're "making it up," this will teach your brain to run the new software of this positive perspective.

When you harness the power of a positive perspective in your own life, you get to make every day a great one!

Until tomorrow,

Paul McKenna

P.S. In just twenty-four hours, we will move forward into the heart of our seven-day adventure—the secret of making your dreams come true. . . .

DAY FOUR

Dreamsetting

Discover what you truly want and
make your dreams come true

BEFORE YOU BEGIN TODAY:

- Listen to the mind-programming session on the CD.
- Take a few minutes to go through the Repro-gramming Your Self-image for Success exercise on page 41.
- Use the power of perspective by asking yourself the power questions from day three:

1. Who or what in your life makes you feel happiest? In answering the question, you will inevitably begin to feel happier. Now let's amplify that feeling—make the images bigger, brighter, and bolder, the sounds louder, and the feelings stronger. Notice where those feelings are strongest and give them a color. Now, move that color and feeling up to the top of your head and down to the tip of your toes until it fills your whole body. . . .

2. Who or what in your life makes you feel most loved? Once again let's amplify that feeling—make the images bigger, brighter, and bolder, the sounds louder, and the feelings stronger. Notice where those feelings are strongest and give them a color. Now, move that color and feeling up to the top of your head and down to the tip of your toes until it fills your whole body. . . .

3. Who or what in your life makes you feel richest? Amplify that feeling of richness—make the images bigger, brighter, and bolder, the sounds louder, and the feelings stronger. Notice where those feelings are strongest and give them a color. Now, move that color and feeling up to the

top of your head and down to the tip of your toes until it fills your whole body. . . .

4. Who or what in your life makes you feel most passionate? Again, amplify the feelings by making the images bigger, brighter, and bolder, the sounds louder, and the feelings stronger. Notice where those feelings are strongest and give them a color. Now, move that color and feeling up to the top of your head and down to the tip of your toes until it fills your whole body. . . .

5. Who or what in your life makes you feel most empowered? You can amplify these feelings of power by making the images bigger, brighter, and bolder, the sounds louder, and the feelings stronger. Notice where those feelings are strongest and give them a color. Now, move that color and feeling up to the top of your head and down to the tip of your toes until it fills your whole body. . . .

6. While you feel this good, think about the rest of the day ahead, feeling and imagining things going perfectly, going the way you want them to go. See what you'll see, hear what you'll hear, and feel how good it feels. As you go through the ritual of building this super state each day, it has a powerful cumulative effect. You will soon begin to experience life in a completely different way. Instead of manipulating the world to make you feel good, you can begin each day feeling the way you want to feel.

Well done! You have once again programmed yourself to have a great day!

A MAN WAS WALKING ALONG A BEACH, reflecting on his life. He had always wanted to make a difference, but no matter what he tried, he wound up feeling as though he was spitting into the wind.

Suddenly, the man heard a loud "crunch" and looked down at his feet. Right where he was standing, and for as far as the eye could see in either direction, there were thousands upon thousands of tiny starfish washed up onto the shore by the ocean waves and tide.

The man continued walking, thinking to himself about the apparent cruelty of the ocean. After all, those starfish hadn't done anything wrong! Yet before the day was done, they would be dead, washed up on shore and left to die.

After a time, the man came across an old woman standing at the ocean's edge, throwing starfish that had washed up on shore back into the sea.

When he asked her what she was doing, she said she had always wanted to make a difference, and she had decided that today was a good day to begin.

The man looked from her to the thousands upon thousands of starfish that lay dying along the coastline and said, "For every starfish you throw back into the ocean, three more wash up onto the shore! How can you possibly be making a difference?"

The woman looked thoughtful for a moment, then she picked up another starfish and threw it back into the sea. "Made a difference to that one," she said, and she smiled the most beautiful smile the man had ever seen.

The Goal of Setting Goals

I'm sure you've heard about the importance of goals before, so at first glance, some of what I'm going to share with you today may seem familiar. You may have even set goals in the past, and gotten all excited about achieving them, only to find your motivation wane when what you set in motion didn't come to pass. Or perhaps you got what you thought you wanted, only to discover it wasn't and were left to reflect, Is this all there is?

But don't be fooled or tempted to skip ahead—today is going to be different. The crucial difference is that this time we're going to put goals in their proper place—as servants of a better life.

Today, you're going to learn a whole new way of thinking about what it is you want in life. Goals are actually the LEAST important part of the three-step process you will learn. Using the amazing techniques in today's lesson, we're going to help you take control of your life and steer it in the direction you want.

> *"The purpose of life is a life of purpose."*
> ROBERT BYRNE

By the time we're finished today, you'll not only be clearer than ever about what it is that you want, you'll also have begun to program your goals and dreams directly into your unconscious mind. This will make them easier to achieve than ever before!

Three Steps to a Wonderful Life

There are essentially only three things you need to have a wonderful life:

1. **A clear direction (your Dream)**

2. **A well-aligned compass (your Values)**

3. **Milestones you can visit along the way to your ultimate destination (your Goals)**

For our purposes, we can think about it like this:

When you pursue your goals guided by your values in the context of your dreams, miracles happen!

Dreamers of the Day

We all have dreams—deeply felt desires for a different, better life. Take a moment now just to fantasize—to let your mind wander, literally to "daydream."

Answer the following question:

What would you do if you knew you couldn't fail?

> *"All men dream, but not all equally. Those who dream by night, in the dusty recesses of their minds, wake to find it was all vanity. But the dreamers of the day are dangerous, for they may act their dreams with open eyes, and make things happen."*
>
> T.E. LAWRENCE

If you paused and considered the question for even a moment, you've just done what all truly successful people throughout history have done—used a purposeful state of daydreaming to access the creative realm.

The great genius Nikola Tesla, inventor of alternating current (AC) and holder of 111 other US patents, could design a machine perfectly in his mind and "operate" it mentally for years before ever creating its counterpart in the physical world. Einstein imagined riding through space on a beam of light to develop his theory of relativity. Mozart heard whole symphonies already completed in his creative mind. Michelangelo, Goethe, and Walt Disney all entered the creative daydream or reverie daily as a source of ideas and inspiration.

What all these innovators were doing was a form of visualization, self-hypnosis, or, as it's known in the corporate world, "strategic planning," which I will be sharing with you later in this chapter. All of us need to engage in this creative activity. In fact, the more time you spend in creative dreaming, the more successful you will become.

Why is this state of creative reverie so important?

Because for anything to happen in the real world it first has to happen in the imaginary world.

Stop reading and look around you—almost everything you can see started as a thought in someone's head. In order for you to improve your life, yourself, or the world, you first need to allow yourself to dream.

Discovering Your "Big Dream"

Viktor Frankl, a famous psychologist, was imprisoned by the Nazis in a concentration camp during World War II. Rather than see himself as a victim of even such exceptional circumstances, he decided instead to make a personal study of what were the psychological differences between the 1 in 28 prisoners who survived the extreme deprivation and the vast majority who did not.

> *"Success, like happiness, cannot be pursued; it must ensue. . . as the unattained side effect of one's personal dedication to a course greater than oneself."*
>
> VIKTOR FRANKL

He observed that those who made it through were not necessarily the fittest, healthiest, or most intelligent, but rather those who had a purpose to live for—a dream of sufficient size, scope, and meaning that they had a burning desire to overcome any obstacle. Dreams were what kept them going.

When the mind has a target, it can focus and direct itself until it reaches its goal. If you have no target, then your energy is dissipated. Yet what you achieve in your pursuit of success is often not as important as who you become in the process. Here's the great secret of our dreams:

When you're working on a truly worthwhile dream, the dream is also working on you.

In the 1960s President John F. Kennedy talked of putting a man on the moon. He told Americans:

"We choose to go to the moon in this decade and do the other things, not because they are easy, but because they are hard—because that goal will serve to organize and measure the best of our energies and skills. Because that challenge is one that we are willing to

accept, one we are unwilling to postpone,
and one which we intend to win."

When asked about the most positive things that came about as a result of America's involvement in the space race, most scientists agree that it was neither the advances in engineering or rocket design nor even the discoveries about the geological formations on the moon.

It was rather the discovery of a cure for smallpox, which came about as a result of research into how to keep the astronauts safe from any diseases they might encounter in space.

Just as going to college isn't about getting a piece of paper, dreamsetting is not just about getting what you want—it's about becoming more than you ever thought you could be.

I do believe that having goals is essential, because they give you a direction in life. You wouldn't set out in a boat without a rudder—you could end up anywhere. We all know those people who leave everything to chance, getting tossed around by life's random events.

I also believe that knowing what your values are is excellent, because happiness comes from living your values every single day, regardless of how close or far away your goals may seem to be.

But just as Viktor Frankl found that people can survive almost anything if they have a purpose, all the truly great achievers in history had this additional factor in common—they had a definite purpose, or dream. And knowing how your goals and values reflect that dream is the key to both success *and* fulfillment.

What if I Don't Know What to Dream?

Studies have shown that less than 3 percent of us write down our goals. We don't bother to design our destiny, preferring to stumble through life, leave things to chance, and wonder why we feel so bad. In fact, most people will spend more time making a list for the supermarket than they will making a list of the really important things they want in life. Yet as John Wooden, the most successful basketball coach in college history, was fond of saying, "If you fail to plan, plan to fail."

> "A goal is nothing more than a dream with a deadline."
> JOE L. GRIFFITH

In essence, all you need to do is to think of something you want, imagine what it would be like to have it, check to see if it's OK for you to have it, think about how it might come about, then focus your mind upon your dream regularly.

Back in the late 1980s I sat down and asked myself, "If I continue along the present course I'm on, where will I end up? Where will I be five years from now?"

I was shocked to realize that if I carried on with my day-to-day habitual patterns of thinking and acting, five years from now I wouldn't really be any more fulfilled, spiritually, emotionally, or financially. I'd just be five years older, a little bit more paranoid, and still living from day to day.

So I took myself through the process I'll be sharing with you today. I did visualizations like the ones at the end of this chapter.

> "The talent is in the choices."
> ROBERT DE NIRO

The results were astounding, and are one of the reasons you're reading this book now. I immediately began to feel better. I suddenly found I had more energy. Opportunities flooded in, my finances took a significant upturn, and I became very well known. I began to attract the kind of people around me who I always wanted to spend time with and do the things I'd always dreamed of doing. Not only were my dreams coming true, but I was finally living a wonderful life.

Based on that experience and many more since

then, here is the seven-step system I use to guide myself and thousands of people on my seminars and trainings to live the lives of our dreams. . . .

The Dreamsetting System

> "Things which matter most must never be at the mercy of things which matter least."
>
> GOETHE

What makes the Dreamsetting System different from traditional goal-setting is that we begin and end with everyone's ultimate goal—living a wonderful life.

In order to do this, it will first be necessary to identify your core values—those things that make your life worth living. These will act as a compass for your journey. Once you are clear on your values, we will identify your "big dream"—that thing that gives you a clear sense of direction and purpose. Finally when your compass is aligned and your direction is clear, we will focus on more traditional goals—the mile markers on the road to your dreams and the building blocks of your wonderful life.

This section of *Change Your Life in 7 Days* may well be the most important of all, so take your time with it. Grab a pen and some paper and take the time to answer the questions in as much detail as possible. Don't worry about "getting it right"—life will reward every sincere effort to make it better!

Step One—The Most Important Things in the World

What would you do if the world was going to end one week from today?

Your answer to that question is the key to identifying your values—those things that matter most in your life. I have worked with a number of people who were at the end of their lives. I asked some of them what they wished they'd done more of and less of. None of them said, "I wish I had another Mercedes."

They said things like, "I wish I'd laughed more and loved more," or, "I wish I had spent less time worrying."

I was shocked recently to hear one motivational speaker exhort his audience to devote twenty-four hours a day to the pursuit of their financial goals. "If your family doesn't understand," he went on, "get a new family." As his fourth wife smiled and nodded at the back of the room, I thought to myself, what good is a successful career if it's at the cost of your marriage and you hardly ever see your children?

The opportunities to live abundantly are all around us, but just acquiring the symbols of success will not make us any happier. When you learn to focus on your values and your life's purpose instead of just your goals, you will automatically begin to take the big picture of your life into account.

In his book *The Power of Full Engagement*, corporate coach Dr. James Loehr offers the following questions to help you get in touch with your core values—the most important things in your world:

1. Jump ahead to the end of your life. What are the three most important lessons you have learned and why are they so critical?

2. Think of someone you deeply respect. Describe three qualities in this person that you most admire.

3. Who are you at your best?

4. What one-sentence inscription would you like to see on your tombstone that would capture who you really were in your life?

Now make a list of the most important things that emerged from answering these questions. Be sure to look beyond any material things on your list to the states of being that lie behind them.

For example, I remember on one of my seminars a man did this exercise and discovered that the most important thing in his world was money. When I asked him what having money would give him, he took some time to imagine himself having lots and lots of the stuff. When he opened his eyes, he said, "Having money will give me a feeling of security, and if I have money, people will respect me." What was really important to him was security and respect—those were the states of being he was pursuing money to try to experience.

Based on your list, choose your top five values—the things on your list you absolutely cannot imagine going without. These five things are the very essence of what will give your life meaning—the most important things in your world.

If you do nothing else but live these values every single day, you cannot imagine how fulfilling your life will become!

Step Two—Brainstorm!

When it comes to your success, you need to become unreasonable. You need to have dreams that are beyond what you and everybody around you thinks of as possible. As George Bernard Shaw said, "The reasonable man adapts himself to the world; the unreasonable one persists in trying to adapt the world to himself. Therefore, all progress depends on the unreasonable man."

> "You want what you want, whether or not you think you can get it."
> ROBERT FRITZ

With your values firmly in mind, make a list of everything (yes, everything!) you want now, have wanted in the past, or can conceive of wanting in the future. Just get everything out of your head and down on paper. It is not necessary to have any intention of actually getting any of these things, nor is it necessary that you believe getting any of the items on your list is possible. No matter how weird or impossible it may seem, all you need to do is write it down!

Take at least five minutes to do this now before moving on to step three. . . .

According to Paul Arden's book *It's Not How Good You Are, It's How Good You Want to Be*,

> *"Don't ask what the world needs—ask what makes you come alive and then go and do that. Because what the world needs is people who have come alive."*
>
> HOWARD MARTIN

Victoria Beckham's dream was not to be better than her mates or even to be a famous singer but to become a world brand. In her own words, she described her dream by saying: "I want to be as famous as Persil Automatic."

Step Three—The Big Dream

Only you know what you truly want out of life—what makes your heart sing. When you are answering the questions below, it's very important that you don't stop to consider whether something is possible or not. Just let the answers flow. . . .

- **What do you love to do so much that you'd pay to do it?**

- **What do you feel really passionate about?**

- **What would you choose to do if you had unlimited resources?**

- **Who are the people or characters from history you most admire, and why?**

Answering these questions will help you to get an overall idea of what your life's purpose is about. It takes off the limitations of your present mind-set and lets you become outrageously creative.

If you feel you want additional clarity, ask yourself the following questions:

- **What did you want to do as a child?**

- **What did you want to be when you grew up?**

- **What would you do if you were guaranteed success?**

Write down whatever comes to mind. You're not committing to anything here, and you can organize your thoughts later. You don't need to be too specific at first, and you don't need to figure out how it's going to happen—just let the creative process continue.

Now, think about all the major areas of your life—family, relationships, career, health, community, and spiritual development.

- **What would you really love to happen?**

- **What would you really like to learn?**

- **What skills do you want to master?**

- **How much money do you want to earn?**

- **What character traits do you want to develop?**

- **What do you want to give back to the world?**

In a few moments, I'm going to ask you to begin to formulate your "big dream." As you do, make sure that your dream is focused on what you do want, not on what you don't.

One thing that all of the unhappy people I have ever worked with have in common is that they know what they *don't* want and they focus on it to the point of obsession. What they haven't yet realized is that you always get more of what you focus on.

For example, some people spend all their time thinking of ways to not be fat! Of course, the problem is that in order to "not" be anything you first have to think about being it. So constantly asking questions like, "Why am I so fat?" and "How can I not be fat any more?" is like continually reinforcing your mind with internal representations of yourself as a fat person.

By comparison, a question like, "How am I going to become fit, healthy, and strong?" focuses your attention on what you want.

When you focus upon what you do want as opposed to what you don't, you are making sensory-rich experiences of what you will see, hear, feel, taste, and smell when you get what you want. By regularly concentrating on what you do want, you will condition your mind to attract more of it to you.

Take at least five minutes to do something completely unrelated to this exercise, then come back and write a "first draft" of your big dream. You can use the following form as a guide.

MY BIG DREAM

The most important things in the world to me are:

1.

2.

3.

4.

5.

If I could be, do, and have anything in the world, I would . . .

Step Four—Measuring Success

In the 1930s, a famous study was done into contributory factors to efficiency in the workplace. A team of social scientists went into factories to assess, among other things, the effect of increased lighting on efficiency in assembly lines. As was the typical procedure of the day, three groups were observed.

The first were given increased lighting as they went about their repetitive assembly tasks; the second were given decreased lighting; the third or "control" group were simply observed going about their work in the usual manner. What happened next confounded the observers.

As expected, the group with increased lighting experienced a measurable increase in efficiency and well-being on the job. However, the increase in efficiency and well-being was almost identically matched in both of the other groups being observed.

> "I never ran 1000 miles. I could never have done that. I run one mile 1000 times."
>
> STU MITTLEMAN, WORLD RECORD HOLDER FOR ULTRA-DISTANCE RUNNING

After further experimentation, the conclusion reached by the research team was that the single most important factor in positively affecting the efficiency and well-being of employees was the feeling that attention was being paid to their efforts.

Here's how my friend life coach Michael Neill puts it:

> **"One of the simplest keys to staying motivated over time is to give yourself every opportunity to experience an**

ongoing sense of progress in the pursuit of your goals. Instead of waiting until you have either achieved your goal or failed, continually look and listen for any sign of progress toward your goal; when you find one, grab onto it with all your heart. Seize on any evidence you can find that you are moving in the right direction and delight in it. Hold it large in your mind. Bask in its glow. Throw it onto your bed and roll around naked in it! More than anything else, it is this ongoing sense of progress that will keep you moving in the direction of your dreams week by week and moment by moment."

Ask yourself:

- **What will you see as you achieve your dream?**

- **What will you hear?**

- **What will you feel, smell, and taste?**

Your answers to these questions will give you a way of knowing if you are getting nearer to or further from your dreams, and will keep you motivated as you begin living the life of your dreams.

Step Five—Overcoming Obstacles

Sometimes we can get so caught up in our excitement over pursuing a dream that we overlook important factors that might interfere with our getting what we want. As you project yourself into the future, ask yourself the following questions to ensure that living your dream will be good for you and doesn't harm others:

- **When I think about this dream, does it seem clear or fuzzy?**

- **Do I feel free in my feelings or restricted?**

- **Is this something I am moving toward or away from?**

- **Is this my dream or some other person's dream for me?**

- **What hidden rewards might there be to not living this dream?**

If your answers to any of these questions raise doubts in your mind, congratulate yourself! You've saved yourself months and possibly even years of struggle by identifying potential problems before they strike.

Now add your success measurements and use what you've learned to refine your big dream until just thinking about it makes your heart sing!

MY BIG DREAM

The most important things in the world to me are:

1.

2.

3.

4.

5.

If I could be, do, and have anything in the world, I would . . .

I will know I am succeeding when:

Step Six—Setting Goals on your Success Timeline

Something amazing happens when you have a timeline of events that need to take place in sequence to lead to your dream—you know when you are on track.

How long do you think it will take for you to be fully living your dream? One year? Six years? A lifetime?

Working back from your dream date, figure out the major steps that will need to take place along the way and write them down. These are your goals—the milestones along the road to the life of your dreams.

Make a list of at least seven goals and a timeline that will let you know you are on the way to living your dream. If you like, vividly live each goal in your imagination, seeing what you'll see, hearing what you'll hear and feeling how good you'll feel as you achieve each step. Most importantly, get a clear big bright image of each goal as if it is already happening now.

1.

2.

3.

4.

5.

6.

7.

Step Seven—Activate Your Resources

Now is the time to begin to explore what it's going to take to live your dream. Again and again, I see people relying on the same one or two resources to bail them out of trouble or propel them forward toward their goals and dreams. Whether it's their charm, their trust fund, or their friends, they have become so habituated to using these resources that they forget what else they have available to them.

When they get stuck, it's not because they've really run out of options, but rather because their habitual "knights in shining armor" aren't working or available to them in this particular situation.

In order to activate your resources and step outside your comfort zone, take some time now to list the myriad resources you have at your command.

Here are some categories to get you started:

1. **Your skills, qualities, gifts, and talents**
Examples: loving, kind, a great dancer, a good negotiator, funny, can drink a mug of beer at once, etc.

2. **Your community**

Examples:

- People you work with

- People you work for

- People who work for you

- Family

- Friends

- Neighbors

- Your "fan club"

- People you went to school with

- People you used to work with

- Customers/clients

3. **Your available cash and credit**

Examples: bank accounts, investments, home equity, business equity, etc.

4. **Your possessions**

Examples: house, computer, car, fax machine,

photocopier, desk, chairs, personal and business success books, etc.

One reason it's important to list our resources is that it forces us to expand our thinking outside our comfort zone. And when you are willing to do what you have never done before, all things become possible!

Putting It All Together

Here's an example of how the whole Dreamsetting System fits together:

MY BIG DREAM

The most important things in the world to me are:

1. *Making a difference*
2. *Happiness*
3. *Loving kindness*
4. *Financial security*
5. *Good health*

If I could be, do, and have anything in the world, I would . . .

Be a fantastically successful entrepreneur whose innovative products revolutionize the wellness industry and enhance thousands of people's lives.

I will know I am succeeding when:

I see myself fit and healthy, driving a nice car, wearing nice clothes, with money in the bank.

I hear people telling me how much our products have enhanced the quality of their lives.

I feel a sense of satisfaction and joy each day.

My Big Dream *continued*

(Example)

KEY GOALS	TIMELINE
1. Research innovative wellness products	Within 3 months
2. Choose a product to sell first	Within 6 months
3. Save enough money to quit my job	Within one year
4. Have at least three products in the works and at least five salespeople	Within 18 months
5. Help develop one completely unique product for enhancing people's lives	Within 3 years
6. Patent my product and market it	Within 5 years
7. Earn a million dollars from my patent and be a recognized leader in the field	Within 10 years

Now it's your turn. Fill in the form on the next page or copy it into a notebook or journal.

MY BIG DREAM

The most important things in the world to me are:

1.

2.

3.

4.

5.

If I could be, do, and have anything in the world, I would . . .

I will know I am succeeding when:

My Big Dream *continued*

KEY GOALS	TIMELINE
1.	
2.	
3.	
4.	
5.	
6.	
7.	

As you'll remember from day two, whenever we do something new we create a neural pathway so we can reaccess that experience again easily. Each time we repeat a particular behavior, we strengthen the associated neural pathway.

This is why it is so important to mentally rehearse success. Most of the top athletes I have worked with played hundreds of successful matches and won thousands of races in their own minds before ever setting foot on the playing field. As you visualize living your dream every day, you will build stronger neural pathways to success.

At the height of his success, Hall of Fame basketball player Larry Bird was filming a cola commercial that called for him to shoot for the basket and miss the shot.

The film crew had to film the shot seven separate times because he couldn't help getting the ball in the basket, even when he was trying to miss!

Here's a simple exercise you can do every day to program your mind for success:

PROGRAM YOUR DIRECTION IN LIFE

1. Stop for a moment and vividly imagine what your life will look like as you are living your dream. What will you see? What will you hear? What will people say to you? What will you say to yourself? As you do this, really imagine living your dream in as much detail as possible. Create a rich internal experience as if you are already living your dream now.

2. Next, we will take everything you have learned about what you want, what really matters to you, and what your biggest dream is, and design them all into your ideal week.

3. How does your week begin? Imagine the kind of people you have around you, the places you go, the things you have. How good do you feel? Where do you go each day? What do you do? Who do you see? What are some of the things that let you know how successful you are?

4. Continue to go through your ideal week until you can imagine every detail vividly. This should be an enjoyable process—if it feels like work, take a break, and come back to it when you can relax completely and indulge your imagination. . . .

Taking Action

Of course, if all you had to do was think about what you wanted and it magically showed up a few moments later, everyone would be driving a Ferrari, living in a mansion, wearing expensive jewelry, and sleeping with beautiful lovers. It would also be chaos! That's why the universe puts one more step in between you thinking of what you want and actually getting it—the action step.

Some people sit around and daydream without ever doing anything. However, by creating a vivid representation of how you ideally want to live your life and focusing on it every day, you will become motivated to take action, and you will know where you are going.

As the saying goes, "The journey of a thousand miles begins with a single step." Think of at least one thing that you can do today that will take you in the direction of living your dream, and do it. Even a small step is fine—for example, a phone call or a little bit of research.

> "You can't build a reputation on what you're going to do. It's simple, fantasize, rehearse, then go out into the world and DO IT!"
> — HENRY FORD

Remember the moment you commit to something, providence moves too, and all sorts of unforeseen incidents and assistance occur. It's as though your commitment becomes a magnet for good things to be drawn to you.

In the words of Goethe:

"Whatever you can do, or dream you can do, begin it. Boldness has genius, magic, and power in it. Begin it now!"

Until tomorrow,

Paul McKenna

P.S. Tomorrow, we'll be exploring the first cornerstone of your wonderful life—abundant health!

DAY FIVE

Healthy Foundations

Creating and maintaining a healthy
body, mind, and spirit

BEFORE YOU BEGIN TODAY:

- Listen to the mind-programming session on the CD.
- Take a few minutes to go through the Reprogramming Your Self-image for Success exercise on page 41.
- Review your purpose, values, and goals from day four. Answer the following questions:

1. How will you live your values throughout the day today?

2. What are three actions you will take that will bring you closer to the achievement of your goals?

3. Imagine you are living 'on purpose'—how will you handle any challenges that might come up throughout the day?

As you continue to program yourself for success, you will find your life becomes more and more of a splendid adventure!

THERE WAS A HUNTER walking through the jungle. Suddenly he saw a tiger, but the tiger saw him too.

He ran as fast as he could to get away and tumbled over a cliff. As he fell he grabbed hold of a tree root. There he swung.

He looked up and saw the tiger looking down on him hungrily. Then he saw another tiger appear beneath him, looking up at him hungrily.

He felt a little dirt fall upon his face. He looked up and saw two mice gnawing through the tree root he was holding onto.

To his right he saw a bee fly to a crevice. There he saw a bees' nest overflowing with honey. He reached out and tasted the honey on his fingers. The honey tasted delicious.

What Is the Number-one Cause of Illness and Disease?

A startling study edited by Dr. Bernard Stewart and recently released in the UK predicts that unless people begin taking responsibility for their health and well-being, global rates of cancer could rise 50 percent to 15 million new cases a year by 2020. The study went on to say that as many as two-thirds of these cases can be prevented and/or cured through "lifestyle changes."

While some of these lifestyle changes are outside the scope of this book, the majority of them can be summed up quite simply:

Limit the amount of toxins you put into your body while simultaneously increasing your body's "stress-hardiness."

Most doctors now agree that the mind has a profound effect upon a person's sense of well-being—certainly nearly everyone knows you can think yourself into being ill. When I was a child, it never ceased to amaze me how many of my classmates would get sick on exam day. These are the same people who are always affected by what I call "cultural hypnosis"—they only have to hear a few people saying, "There's a cold going around" and they catch it.

Research has shown that optimists generally live longer, happier, healthier lives. One of the key reasons is because optimum emotional states enhance our immune system. Studies in recent years have now irrefutably proven that we can dramatically enhance our immune systems by actively choosing our beliefs and consistently practicing visualization techniques.

But if the secret of health is a positive perspective, what's causing all the illness and disease?

Let's get right to the point:

The single biggest cause of ill-health is an inappropriate response to stress.

> "What is it that heals a cut finger? Is it the bandage or whatever ointment is applied to the wound? Of course not; it's the body. The human body is self-repairing, self-healing, and self-maintaining."
>
> HARVEY DIAMOND

Studies have shown that the major threat in modern life is being killed by our own defense system being triggered too often—by our response to stress.

What Is Stress?

According to the dictionary, stress is:

a: a constraining force or influence;

b: a force exerted when one body or body part presses on, pulls on, pushes against, or tends to compress or twist another body or body part;

c: a physical, chemical, or emotional factor that causes bodily or mental tension and may be a factor in disease causation.

However, the stress we experience in our own lives does not come from outside us—it is our body's response to life's challenges, both real and imagined. This stress response is historic, as our ancestors needed extreme physical reactions and a burst of energy to enable them to fight a wild animal or run away. Even now, a certain amount of stress in our lives helps us to function—the appropriate arousal of the autonomic nervous system actually motivates us to do things like get out of the way of an oncoming vehicle, or add energy to a presentation or workout.

For example, when the mind perceives a threat, the heartbeat immediately quickens. Pupils dilate automatically, muscles tighten, and adrenaline is released into the bloodstream. The digestive process halts, your blood pressure rises, and the immune system is suppressed. This is known as the "fight or flight" response.

Now, if you are about to be attacked (say by a saber-toothed tiger), you need energy and adrenaline to respond appropriately to the situation. The problem arises when we are continually preparing for emergencies that never happen. This puts an unnecessary strain on our immune systems, ultimately "burning out" our adrenal glands and spreading nasty toxins in the body.

I'll say it again:

The continual *inappropriate* arousal of our mind and body can lead to illnesses.

And although this so-called "negative stress" used to be considered something that affected only people in highly pressured jobs, the truth is that to some degree it affects nearly all of us. And killing ourselves to stay safe is like burning down the house to roast a pig.

These days we do not have to be constantly on the lookout

> "My life has been full of terrible misfortunes, most of which never happened."
> MICHEL DE MONTAIGNE

for wild animals, but the twenty-first century is full of threats from all kinds of different sources. Any average day has its demands and stresses—driving to work there's a traffic jam, you get into an argument, you receive an unexpected bill, the kids have made a mess, you are criticized at work.

These things may not consciously seem like threats to you, but your nervous system does not differentiate between a physical threat to your body and a mental threat to your ego. Research has shown that most worries are either about things that never happen or about things from the past that can't be changed.

In fact, a lot of worry comes down to not having given your mind something better to do. Obviously it's important to have an emotional dynamic range, and if someone's attacking you then you might need to get angry or scared to defend yourself, but what I'm saying is the stress response is being unnecessarily aroused all day long and this builds up over time, causing problems.

The first researcher of the physiological consequences of stress, Hans Selye, remarked that,

"The most important stresses for man are emotional . . . it is not the event but rather our interpretation of it that causes our emotional reaction."

By bringing a positive perspective to our lives and interpreting our experiences differently we can begin to respond beneficially to the events in our life, rather than chaotically.

Whenever you've felt bad in your life, it was a product of your own stress response. That is why in our culture some people turn to alcohol, cigarettes, or drugs to change the way they feel—to cope with stress. As continual negative stress can lead to diseases, it is a problem that needs to be dealt with.

> "If you want to know what your thoughts were like yesterday then check how your body feels today."
>
> INDIAN PROVERB

So Should I Just Avoid Stress?

Any study into the effects of stress on well-being and human performance can usefully be broken down into three areas—stress exposure, stress response, and stress capacity.

Most programs dealing with stress management focus on a combination of the first two factors—reducing stress exposure ("downshifting") and developing a more efficient stress response (relaxation training, meditation, etc.). Yet of the three factors, stress capacity is the most significant in predicting long-term wellness and success.

The greater our capacity to handle stress, the more often we will perform at the peak of our abilities, particularly in high-pressure situations. How do we develop our stress capacity?

Simple—we systematically increase our stress exposure, while balancing our efforts with what stress and performance specialist Dr. James Loehr calls "quality recovery time."

The formula looks like this:

Increased stress exposure
+ Quality recovery time
= Greater stress capacity

Let's take a common example. When you work out your body, you are deliberately putting it under stress. To maximize the effectiveness of your workouts, you need to allow your body time to recover. Every time your muscles (including your heart, in the case of aerobic exercise) are put under stress and then allowed time to recover, they grow stronger.

> *"Don't wish it was easier—wish you were tougher."*
> JIM ROHN

Why do marathon runners and triathletes put such a heavy emphasis on interval training? Because it follows the same pattern. By alternating between periods of intense activity, such as sprinting or racing (stress exposure), and gentle activity, such as walking or coasting (recovery time), they systematically develop their strength and stamina (stress capacity).

Oscillating between stress exposure and recovery is not just a good idea, it is an inevitability. The most extreme example of this can be found in Japan, where *karoshi*, or death from overworking, has at times threatened to become a national epidemic. While death may be the ultimate in quality recovery time, job burnout, exhaustion, and "mysterious illnesses" that keep us from working are the more familiar ways we unconsciously fulfill our body's need for balance.

Here are some simple techniques that you can use to diminish stress and increase your stress hardiness. . . .

1. Power nap

Recent research has shown that the mind and body have their own pattern of rest and alertness with one predominant cycle that occurs approximately every ninety minutes. This is when the body stops externally orientated behavior and takes about fifteen minutes to relax and replenish its energy.

This has become known as the ultradian rhythm.

It's those moments when you find yourself day-dreaming and a gentle, sweet, soft feeling is present in your body. It is quite simply the body's own natural stress-control mechanism.

Unfortunately, many people ignore this message from their body that it is time to relax a little, and instead they have another cup of coffee or try even harder to concentrate. After a while they establish a pattern of overriding the ultradian rhythm.

In future, whenever you find yourself daydreaming and a feeling of comfort starting in your body, go with it and allow yourself to really relax for ten to fifteen minutes. You will then arouse yourself feeling refreshed and with better concentration afterward.

You can deepen this experience even further by practicing self-hypnosis, meditation, or using the CD with this book. I often relax into a trance and imagine myself sunbathing on an exotic beach. Given that the nervous system does not differentiate between a real and a vividly imagined event, when I awaken from a trance like that I feel as though I have just been on holiday—and as far as my nervous system is concerned, I have.

Famous "Nappers"

Thomas Edison and Salvador Dali were both prodigious nappers who used an interesting variation of the power nap to recharge their mental and physical batteries.

They would sit in their favorite chair by the fire while holding a spoon or other metal object in their hand.

As their bodies drifted off toward sleep, the hand holding the spoon would relax, dropping the spoon to the ground.

As soon as they heard the clatter of the metal spoon on the hard wood floor, they would arise refreshed!

The great thing about recharging your batteries with power naps is that you can do it anywhere—after a bit of practice, no one will notice. If you do it on the bus or the train everyone will just think you are dozing.

The following exercise is the version of power napping I use most days—it doesn't take long and it is a good habit to establish that will reinforce all your other stress-reducing efforts. Even if you work in an open-plan office or factory you can always find an excuse to get out for five minutes—remember, repetition is the mother of success!

THE POWER NAP

Do this once or twice a day to give yourself recovery time and improve your well-being.

1. Begin by moving your attention down to your feet. Notice the feelings of your feet, their relative warmth or coolness, and their weight.

2. Take a deep breath in, then let it out, and as you do so imagine a pleasant, warm, and relaxing feeling developing in your feet.

3. Now take another deep, gentle breath in and imagine that warm and relaxing feeling traveling up the legs to your knees. Say the number "one" in your mind.

4. Allow that warm and relaxing feeling to penetrate your muscles and bones, gently spreading and soothing as it moves.

5. When you are ready, take another gentle deep breath and imagine that warm relaxing feeling rising up to your waist, and as it does so say, "two."

6. Breathing in, pull the feeling of ease and relaxation up to your shoulders, and say, "three."

7. Let the relaxation flow up your body to your shoulders and then down along your arms to your hands.

8. Breathing in, let the feeling go all the way, right to the top of your head. Say "four" and spread those good, relaxing feelings all over your body.

9. Now, say in your mind the number "five" and

imagine that relaxing feeling doubling, as if a new, fresh flow of relaxation was descending from above your head and joining the warm relaxing feelings already going on inside you.

10. And as you imagine this flow of relaxation spreading back down your body, imagine any and all tension being washed down along with it, draining out of your body through the bottoms of your feet, making room for you to be refilled on each breath with new, relaxing, refreshing energy. Make sure you take a few moments to really enjoy those feelings of relaxation.

11. Pause for a little while to notice the feeling and then, if you wish, repeat the sequence. The more you practice the technique the more effective it becomes.

Stay with this feeling as long as you wish. If at this point your attention wanders or you would like to close your eyes, that's perfectly OK—you will arise refreshed and alert in just a few minutes. . . .

2. Essential exercise

As we have already seen, the body does not distinguish between an emotional threat and a physical one. So regardless of what happens, it prepares to protect itself by fighting or running away—but often there is no one to fight and nowhere to run to. The body gets worked up but cannot find a way to release its tension.

Fortunately, just as the mind influences the body, so the body can influence the mind. When you find a way to help your body release the tension of the stress response, it feels calmer, safer, and healthier. That in turn affects your mood, making you emotionally clearer and more able to function well—to concentrate, to relax, and to sleep soundly.

The simplest way to help the body release the excess tension of the stress response is to use up the energy and alertness for action that it has prepared—in other words, to get some exercise.

> "All ten studies confirmed that exercise significantly reduces mild to moderate depression. And the three studies that compared exercise to psychotherapy found that exercise was at least as effective."
>
> CONSUMER REPORTS ON HEALTH

Now, before you throw up your hands in horror, realize that your exercise doesn't have to be anything extreme. If you are not used to exercise, even a brisk walk will be helpful. The point is to use up the excess tension and energy flowing through your body and to trigger the body's natural impulse toward rest, relaxation, and recuperation, also known as the parasympathetic response.

The parasympathetic response is the sweet, soft feeling you get in your muscles when you have finished some heavy work or vigorous movement. You also feel a natural high caused by the release of endorphins, the body's natural opiates. (We'll talk more about these on day seven.)

While much has been discussed in the last twenty years about the value of aerobic exercise in increasing our general fitness levels, studies have shown that it is equally important in controlling stress. Swimming, running, or any exercise that oxygenates the blood makes controlling stress easier.

So, even before you master the patterns of thinking and feeling that you have learned thus far in the program, you can give yourself a simple, easy, positive boost by simply having ten to fifteen minutes of brisk exercise each and every day.

3. Energetic eating

Literally thousands of books have been written on what constitutes a healthy diet, many of which directly contradict one another. In order to more easily navigate the volumes of information and misinformation that fill bookshops, libraries, and the Internet, I suggest following one simple rule:

Learn to listen to your body.

In a fascinating experiment performed in the 1930s, scientists gave a group of toddlers unlimited 24/7 access to a vast range of foods from ice cream to spinach, essentially allowing them to create their own diet over a period of thirty days based on nothing more than their own sense of what they wanted to eat and when.

The result?

Despite variations in timing, sequence, and frequency, every child in the study wound up choosing what was considered to be a "balanced" diet over the course of the month. As we learn to listen to the wisdom of our bodies, we too can experience the benefits of optimal health.

The fact is, some foods increase your vitality and well-being; other foods diminish it. Author and researcher Dr. Gay Hendricks recommends the following exercise to determine which foods are your personal high-energy foods:

Step one: Eat a food you like.

Step two: Notice your body sensations 45–60 minutes later. If you feel clear and energetic, you ate a high-energy food for you. If you don't, you didn't!

In Dr. Hendricks' research, he discovered that when people felt energized an hour after eating, that feeling of energy tended to stay with them for several more hours, usually until the next time they needed to eat.

By practicing this simple exercise for as little as a week, you can custom-design a perfect diet for your own unique body!

4. Medicinal laughter

Recent research has shown that healthy people are usually happy people. That's why a good sense of humor is so important. Having a sense of humor is vital, not just to amuse your-self at parties, but as an essential psycho-logical resource. When you are "light-hearted," your body manufactures

"Dr. Lee S. Berk . . . conducted his own scientific research into the connection between the laughing brain and the immune system. Blood tests were carried out on selected control groups before and after a mirth-making activity, such as watching a funny film. The results saw an increase in the numbers of natural killer cells (NK cells), which are important for the immune system.

"Every day, cells in our body undergo a lot of change, creating potential carcinogenic cells," says Berk. "NK cells destroy these aberrant cells and are therefore significant in terms of immunosurveillance. . . .

That doesn't mean that a doctor is going to tell you to take two aspirins and watch Laurel and Hardy, but the reality is that now there's a real science to the health benefits of laughter. And it's as real as taking a drug."

FROM *THE GUARDIAN*,
MARCH 25, 2003

different chemicals inside you than those it manufactures when you are unhappy.

In *Anatomy of an Illness*, Norman Cousins writes his account of using laughter to help control his pain and ultimately heal his body of ankylosing spondylitis, a degenerative illness that at the time was considered irreversible in 499 out of 500 cases. Not only did Cousins recover, he went on to live in excellent health for another twenty-five years.

Research has shown that when we smile we release serotonin, otherwise know as "happy chemicals," in the brain. So while "laughing yourself healthy" is still seen as radical therapy here in the West, consider the fact that the Taoists have been using the power of the "inner smile" as a healing tool for more than 2,500 years!

I first came across the practice of the inner smile I am going to share with you now in the works of modern-day Taoist master Mantak Chia, who wrote:

*"Taoist Sages say that when you smile,
your organs release a honey-like secretion
which nourishes the whole body. When
you are angry, fearful, or under stress,
they produce a poisonous secretion
which blocks up the energy channels."*

The practice of the inner smile I share on the following pages is the way I use it to release tension and promote ease and well-being in my own body.

THE INNER SMILE

1. Sit comfortably—ultimately, you can practice the inner smile anywhere, in any position.

2. Allow a smile to dance into your eyes. If you like, raise the corners of your mouth ever so slightly, like someone who knows a really cool secret but doesn't need to tell.

3. Smile into any part of your body that feels tight, or uncomfortable, until it begins to ease or relax.

4. Smile into any part of your body that feels especially good. You can increase the smile by expressing gratitude to that part of your body for helping to keep you healthy and strong.

5. Allow the inner smile to reach every corner of your body. Here are some specific suggestions:

   a. Smile into the organs of your body—your heart, liver, pancreas, kidneys, sex, and adrenal glands. If you don't know where these organs are, it's OK to pretend—your body will redirect the energy for you.

   b. Smile down through your esophagus and into your stomach. Smile all the way through your large and small intestines and out of your bottom. (If anyone can think of a more delicate way to put that, answers on a postcard, please!)

   c. Smile up into your brain, then down through

> the base of your skull, and all the way down to the bottom of your spine.
>
> You can smile into your life as well as your body. Try smiling and expressing gratitude into a relationship, an environment, or a project you are currently working on, and notice how the energy around that situation begins to shift!

5. Believe yourself well

A few years ago some interesting research was conducted to try to discover why a small number of people survive cancer while the vast majority of people do not. The study interviewed a hundred people who had at one time been diagnosed as terminally ill but were still alive at least twelve years after the initial diagnosis was made.

WHY CAN'T I JUST TAKE PRESCRIPTION DRUGS TO REDUCE MY STRESS?

As they say in Alcoholics Anonymous, your body can't tell the difference between a prescription drug and one bought on a street corner.

There are also other ways to improve your health. These days there are many reports about what's bad for us, but let's not forget one very important thing. We all have our own immune system: the body and mind working together to heal, protect, and regulate the fantastic vessel that we essentially are. We live in an age when incredible medical advancements are constantly taking place. Drugs and surgery have become commonplace. Many people expect instant cures from the doctors for their ills and hand over responsibility for their health to the medical profession, preferring a prescription to instigating a change in their lifestyle or diet.

The cultural acceleration of use of prescription drugs has led to other problems. Dr. E.W. Marting believes that more people are killed each year by prescribed drugs in the U.S. and Britain than are killed in road accidents. Perhaps this is one reason why so many people are looking to alternative ways to improve their health.

The intention of the study was to discover any patterns of thinking or behavior shared by these long-term survivors. The results were startling but conclusive. While they had all used different treatments, ranging from surgery and chemotherapy to acupuncture and natural diets, and some had even relied on purely psychological techniques or religious practices, all one hundred people shared one essential trait:

They believed that what they were doing would work for them.

In medical history, there is an interesting demonstration of the power of belief known as "the placebo effect." A placebo is a tablet with no inherent curative properties. Because the United States requires all new drugs to be tested against placebos, there's an unusual amount of research on them.

On average, placebos are about 30 percent as effective as a medical drug. However, in some specific cases their effectiveness is much higher. Compared against morphine, placebos are 54 percent as effective, even though morphine is considered a class A narcotic.

We are only beginning to understand the incredible power of hypnosis and its possible role in medicine and therapy in the future. Some doctors have recently proved how just using the imagination can affect your health. Other research has shown that people who believe they can control their immune system find that they can easily do so by using hypnotic or guided imagery techniques. Many individuals could actually increase the number of protective blood cells in their bodies almost at will, instantly improving their resistance to illness.

In a related study, two doctors at Yokohama City University in Japan demonstrated that 84 percent of subjects could eliminate the standard histamine response to poison ivy. The itching, swelling, and blisters disappeared when the subjects under hypnosis simply imagined the poison ivy to be a harmless plant. Just as important in our understanding of the impact of the mind on wellness, a large number of subjects broke out in blisters when they reversed the experiment and imagined the harmless plant to be poison ivy.

As a result of these and other studies like them, most health-care professionals now acknowledge that a patient's attitude is a major factor in the success of their recovery.

But What if I'm "Really" Sick?

Another amazing experiment, conducted by Dr. David Spiegel at Stanford University, examined a group of women with breast cancer. While everyone in the group received the latest medical treatment for their illness, one half of the group also learned self-hypnosis and did very simple guided imagery, imagining themselves relaxed and floating. After a year, the group that had learned to relax and imagine themselves relaxed reported much less pain and more optimism.

What really surprised the researchers didn't emerge until much later. Ten years after the initial experiment was conducted, members of the second half had lived an average of twice as long as the first. While nobody is saying that hypnosis is a cure for cancer, regular self-hypnosis or guided imagery will clearly improve the quality of your life, and may well have a positive effect on the length of it.

One of the first terminally ill people I ever worked with was a lady who had cancer. Each time she had chemotherapy her immune system became depleted, which left her feeling low, both physically and mentally. Her doctor had explained to her that it usually takes about two weeks for the immune system to return to normal after the type of chemotherapy she was having, but once she learned the simple visualization technique that I will share with you in a few moments, her system was completely rejuvenated after just five days. The doctor could hardly believe it.

A less serious but equally dramatic example was an actress friend of mine who noticed she was getting a cold sore, which normally would last for up to five days. She was due to begin filming later that evening. She relaxed her body, then visualized herself using the immune-system booster each day for five days, crossing the days off a mental calendar one at a time. Five "inner days" later, she visualized the cold sore gone. When she came back out of relaxed visualization or trance, the "tingle" that usually signified the imminent onset of a cold sore had disappeared, and it never came back.

My inspiration for the immune-system booster came from an experiment carried out by Professor Karen Olness at the Rainbow Babies and Children's Hospital of University Hospitals in Cleveland. The experiment involved a group of children being shown a video featuring puppets. One puppet represented a virus; another, which looked like a policeman, represented the immune system. The video was a simplified illustration of the internal workings of the body that the children could easily understand.

When the video finished the children were told to close their eyes, relax, and imagine lots of policemen puppets running around their bodies. Saliva samples were then taken from each child and the results showed that their immunoglobulin levels had substantially increased—that is, their immune systems had begun working as though they were fighting off real infections.

I began wading through the clinical research in a relatively new area known as psychoneuroimmunology, or PNI. There, I found masses of irrefutable evidence confirming that it's possible to boost your immune system just by thinking about it in certain ways. The idea behind PNI is that our body knows how to repair itself and maintain perfect holistic health. Programmed into your immune system is the ability to recognize those cells that belong to you and those that are invaders from the outside that must be destroyed or appropriately consumed.

Once your immune system comes in contact with bacteria, a virus, or an abnormal cell, it will never forget the encounter. During its first exposure, your immune system produces targeted "biochemical weapons" designed to combat that specific abnormal "invader." Your immune system is strong and intelligent enough to control and coordinate its actions so that you effortlessly maintain a state of healthy vitality.

The Immune-System Booster

A normal, healthy immune system is a wonderful thing and has almost miraculous healing powers. But those powers can be enhanced through the application of the simple visualization I will be sharing with you.

Here's a letter I received recently from a man who used these techniques to make a dramatic difference in his own life and in the lives of others:

Dear Paul,

About five years ago, I received the worst news I could have feared. A successful sales executive, I had been troubled by strange bouts of dizziness, numbness, and slurring. At one sales presentation, I had even been struck dumb in mid-sentence. After extensive medical tests, the neurologist gave the dreadful diagnosis "Multiple sclerosis" (MS), the incurable and degenerative nerve disease. The news came as a hammer-

blow. My dreams for the future were swept away, and the doctors told me to brace myself for "managed decline"—the heartless, clinical term for the inexorable slide into dependency, disease, and death. I was encouraged to go away and cry as I needed to come to terms with my plight. Two exacerbations of the disease in the space of two months indicated to my neurologist that MS was very active in my body and his view was that this was likely to bring about my swift decline.

However, after six months of the deepest despair, my attitude toward this disease changed and I began to move toward hope. I transformed my way of life—starting with a radical change of diet, and reaching into my deepest philosophical and spiritual attitudes. The catalyst for this change was your CD Supreme Self-Confidence. I noticed that from somewhere within a newfound hope surged. In my mind's eye I created a positive and vibrant self-image that I moved toward with increasing confidence. One year after my diagnosis, I was back to my optimum weight; and

I was even back playing rugby again.
This was a positive reinforcement of my
new healthy invigorated self-image.

I am now in the best physical and
mental health of my life. I continue to
harness the power of my unconscious
mind as my life and health continue
to flourish. Amazingly, five years after
the evening I first listened to your CD,
I have not had a single exacerbation
of MS and I have been completely
symptom-free for more than four years.

People like me—hopeless cases, as
judged by western medical standards—
are living proof that the power of the
unconscious mind has profound lessons
for us all. For me healing others is now
more than just a mission—it is also an
amazing adventure in life, and in living.

Whether you're as healthy as an ox or you're currently experiencing symptoms of unwellness, take a
few minutes now to try the following technique:

IMMUNE-SYSTEM BOOSTER

Please note: this technique is not intended as a substitute for medical treatment, although it may be used in conjunction with treatments prescribed by your physician.

1. Close your eyes and imagine your immune system in a way that appeals to you. My personal preference is to think of it as lots of light-colored jellyfish-type creatures, which is similar to how the protective cells actually look. Make sure there are plenty of them and see them as strong and purposeful.

2. Next, imagine traveling inside your body to the area that needs healing and notice how you imagine the problem manifesting. You might see the infection or diseased cells as lots of tiny black jelly globules.

3. In your mind, see the big light-colored jellyfish encapsulating and devouring the little black globules.

4. When the little black globules are gone, it's very important to then imagine the light jellyfish happily swimming and patrolling your bloodstream. This is to ensure that you do not overstimulate your immune system.

5. Now imagine a healthier you standing or sitting in front of you. See how the healthier you looks, breathes, smiles, etc.

6. Finally, step into the healthier you, see through the eyes of the healthier you, hear through the ears, and feel how much better you feel!

By now, I'm sure you've begun to realize your amazing potential for health, energy, and well-being. Return to the ideas and exercises in this chapter as often as you like to unleash that potential and energize one of the cornerstones of wealth—your physical body! Until tomorrow,

Paul McKenna

P.S. Tomorrow, we'll take a look at another cornerstone of wealth and the key to a happy, healthy life— the ability to create money from every opportunity!

DAY SIX

Creating Money

Discovering the secrets of the millionaire's mind

BEFORE YOU BEGIN TODAY:

- Listen to the mind-programming session on the CD.

- Take a few minutes to go through the Reprogramming Your Self-image for Success exercise on page 41.

- Review your purpose, values and big dream from day four.

- If you need more energy, guide yourself through the natural relaxation exercise in day five.

- Choose your favorite exercise from days two and three to create a great state and program your day!

IN DAYS GONE BY, there was a wealthy man who had a wonderful steamship, but as is the way with expensive things, it was prone to breaking down. One day, after a particularly difficult journey to a foreign land, the engine failed and no one could get it going again.

One by one, every mechanic and engineer in the land was summoned to try to fix the engine, and one by one they failed. Finally, word came to the wealthy man of a wise old shipmaker who might be able to help, but at a hefty price. The wealthy man agreed at once.

Soon, an old man who looked as if he must have been fixing ships for a hundred years arrived. He carried a large bag of tools and immediately went to work. He inspected the large network of pipes leading to and from the engine very carefully, occasionally placing his hand upon the pipes to test for warmth.

Finally, the old shipmaker reached into his bag and pulled out a small hammer. He gently tapped against one of the pipes. Instantly, the sound of steam rushing through the pipes could be heard and the engine lurched to life as the shipmaker carefully put his hammer away.

When the wealthy man asked the shipmaker what he owed him, the bill came to more than ten thousand dollars—a princely sum in those days.

"What?" the wealthy owner exclaimed, outraged. "You hardly did anything at all! Justify your bill or I will have you thrown into jail."

The old shipmaker began to scrawl something onto a ragged

piece of paper he pulled from his pocket. The wealthy man smiled as he read it and apologized to the shipmaker for his rude behavior.

This is what it said:

| For tapping with a hammer | $1 |
| For knowing where to tap | $9999 |

The Wealth of the World

You are one of the wealthiest people who has ever lived. Now, I don't know you, of course, but I can still safely make my assertion because our modern culture is so much wealthier than any previous society in the history

> "Lack of money is the root of all evil."
> GEORGE BERNARD SHAW

of mankind. In fact, when I walk down the street in almost any city I visit, I'm struck by how much wealth there is in the world and how few of us are truly aware of it.

Real wealth isn't just about money—it's about your access to resources, whether or not those resources technically belong to you. The Indian guru Swami Muktananda, upon arriving in America for the first time, stood in the airport and said:

"They live in paradise, yet they will never know it." Just think about what you have accessible to you even if you have virtually no money at all—beautiful streets and parks to walk through, libraries, more music, film, theatre, and sports than ever before, schools for your children, and hospitals for your body. In short, things that were only available to the privileged elite a few short centuries ago probably feel like your birthright.

Real wealth is about having an abundance of good health and true happiness. It's about having good friends or family who you can share intimate and pleasurable experiences with and laugh with, people who stimulate and fascinate you. Real wealth is feeling happy most of the time. It's a sense of knowing you are contributing something to the world, and that your life is worthwhile. After all you are unique—nobody can do things exactly the way you do them.

Of course, wealth is also partly about having money. And today we are going to focus very specifically and very deliberately on that one thing— money.

All About Money

The earliest system of trade was bartering. Coins were the first officially sanctioned IOUs, used to represent the value of things in the world. Then came paper money. A banknote or a dollar bill is essentially an IOU from the government. Until recently, they used to print only as many notes and bills as they had gold reserves to back up.

However, in the 1940s the governments of the world decided to abandon the gold standard system. Since then, they have been printing money as if it was going out of fashion. Now, the gold in reserve is only a fraction of the amount of paper money in circulation, and even paper money is being replaced by plastic credit cards and numbers in computers.

So money is essentially a symbol of value—that is, it represents value although it has no inherent value of its own. Since our money is no longer backed by gold, why do we still act as if it's worth something?

Because of our confidence or faith in the source of the money, in this case, the government that issued it. This leads us to a simple yet radical way of thinking about money:

Money is a symbol of our confidence in our product, our service, and ourselves!

Here's how author Serge Kahili King puts it:

"People can fail, too, when [we] lose confidence in them or when they lose confidence in themselves, regardless of the value of their goods and services.

*Likewise, people can succeed when
people have extraordinary confidence in
them or when they have extraordinary
confidence in themselves, also regardless
of the value of their good and services. . . .*

*"If you want to have more money in your
life—for yourself or to help others or
both—then you have to make yourself
more valuable in the eyes of other people.
It won't be enough to provide valuable
goods and services, or to be in the right
place at the right time, or even to pick
the right numbers. You'll have to be more
spiritual than that. You'll have to have
more faith, more confidence, in your own
value, as a provider or as a person."*

This reveals the magic formula for making more
money:

**The more confidence we have in ourselves and/or our
product or service, the more we will be able to charge for it.**

And here's the really good news: if money is confidence, and confidence is a state, then you already
have everything it takes to make all the money you

could ever possibly want—you just have to choose to cultivate it!

How I Became a Millionaire

Before I started using the techniques I will be sharing with you in this chapter, I was in debt, living from day to day in a tiny room I rented in someone else's apartment. I had a small circle of friends, a job I didn't really like, and it was an effort to get myself up and out of bed in the morning.

Within a few months, I had completely transformed my financial situation. I made more money in those few months than I had in the previous few years. This new pattern in my life started a chain reaction, and I began creating money everywhere I looked. I developed an amazingly successful second career, the success of which is probably why you're reading this book, and my circle of friends expanded to include people who I'm proud to number among my friends nearly two decades later. Within a few years, I had become a millionaire.

What's fascinating is that until that point, I had always believed that in order to make money I had to go out into the world and get it from

> *"If someone hands you a million dollars, best you become a millionaire, or you won't get to keep the money."*
>
> JIM ROHN

other people. Instead, as I changed myself and my perception of the world, money began flowing to me. After a few more years had passed, I began teaching others the principles of how I had created abundance in my life, and very quickly their lives transformed too. Now, I'm going to share those same secrets with you!

How to Overcome Poverty Consciousness

Research has shown that a massive proportion of those who get sudden large sums of money, for example, from lotteries or inheritance, are almost guaranteed to lose it all very quickly. In fact, 80 percent are actually worse off financially just two years later. That's because inside they still feel poor.

In psychology, this is referred to as "the Pygmalion effect" or the "self-fulfilling prophecy," which I've talked about already. What we expect to be true in our minds will tend to become true in reality. Even if our expectations aren't initially accurate, we act in ways that are consistent with our expectations. Those actions then create the results we expected, and the "prophecy" of our expectations is fulfilled.

> *"You can't help the poor by being one of them."*
> ABRAHAM LINCOLN

If you believe you can't really become wealthy, you will speak and act consistently with that belief and in most cases "prove" yourself right. Similarly, if you change your expectations of the world to reflect your infinite potential for wealth, you will quickly generate the thoughts, feelings, and behaviors that will draw money to you.

Our culture is continually programming us with negative financial associations. We have been taught things like, "The Bible says 'Money is the root of all evil.'" What the Bible actually says is, "The *love* of money is the root of all evil"—that is, the acquiring of money for its own sake, as a commodity to be hoarded.

Or we are told that there is only a finite amount of wealth and that the more we have, the less there will be for others. Or that "all rich people are liars and thieves." (It's common in our culture to hear terms such as "filthy rich" or "fat cat," which are indicative of an underlying mistrust of people with money.)

Many of these limiting ideas about money are

historically derived. During the Middle Ages, the feudal system kept wealth in the hands of the privileged few, while the masses were tricked into believing that poverty was their salvation. This hierarchical system of power worked on the assumption that there is only a finite amount to go around, implying a scarcity of wealth. Poverty was glamorized by the Church, and for many years it was actually considered a Christian virtue to be poor, with monks having to take a vow of poverty to be initiated into their order.

Some people who grew up in the last century during the Depression, or experienced the rationing of food and essentials during World War II, still carry an unconscious belief that "there just won't be enough to go around." And many of them have unconsciously passed these limiting beliefs on to their children.

Even if you believe some of these things are true, it is important that you recognize the inherent problem:

If you believe money is bad in some way, you will unconsciously sabotage your attempts to create more of it in your life.

I've found that most wealthy, successful people tend to share the same simple habits and beliefs about prosperity. However, I believe that many people unknowingly use this same powerful principle to keep themselves poor, through the beliefs and habits they have toward money.

Instead of taking responsibility for their beliefs and actions (and therefore their wealth), they use their lack of money as "proof" that they are meant to be poor. They have affirmed their poverty over and over so many times that it unwittingly became a self-fulfilling prophecy, a poverty consciousness.

This is not to say that if you are poor, it is in any way your fault. We are not responsible for the hand we are dealt, but we can and must take full responsibility for how we play that hand.

For example, some artists believe that they cannot have commercial success, because it would "compromise their artistic integrity." Other people believe that you can't be a good person unless you are always putting others first, even if it's to your own detriment. Some people stay poor because it feels safer—it's what they know.

As you use the Change Your Life in 7 Days system you are going to let go of any old limiting ideas you had about money and reprogram your mind to become more prosperous and think like a millionaire. Here are two mental "laws" that explain why some people become stuck in a never-ending loop of poverty while others seem to turn everything they touch to gold.

1. The Law of Reversed Effort

One of the most important ideas in hypnosis is called "the law of reversed effort." It can be summed up in the pop psychology phrase:

What you resist persists.

Some people have deep-rooted beliefs that keep them poor. For one reason or another they sabotage themselves getting rich. No matter how hard they try consciously to get rich their unconscious beliefs will not support them and they end up sabotaging themselves.

Yet the law of reversed effort teaches us that if deep down you think of yourself as poor, you'll constantly fear poverty. Since what you focus on you get more of, poverty is usually exactly what you'll get.

The exception to that rule is people who are driven to accumulate money by their

> "A particular train of thought persisted in, be it good or bad, cannot fail to produce its results in the character and circumstances.
>
> "A man cannot directly choose his circumstances, but he can choose his thoughts, and so indirectly, yet surely, shape his circumstances."
>
> JAMES ALLEN, AS A MAN THINKETH

fear of poverty. I've met and gotten to know some of the richest people in the world, but some of them have very little of what I'd call real wealth—workaholics, driven to look for their next million at the cost of time for family or friends. They are driven by a fear of poverty, and no matter how much money they accumulate, it will never be enough.

Obviously a concern for organized finances is not the same as a dread of poverty. But that deep-rooted fear of poverty is how some people manage to amass huge riches without ever getting out of the trap of poverty consciousness.

2. The Law of Attraction

Have you ever thought about someone and, moments later, the phone rings and it's them? How did you explain that to yourself? Was it telepathy? Coincidence? Magnetic attraction? Or perhaps you were thinking about getting a particular car and then suddenly began seeing that type of car everywhere. How did you explain that?

The Law of Attraction states:

What you focus on consistently, you get more of in your life.

If you focus on poverty and lack, you will tend to get more of that in your life. If you focus on the wealth that is already there, you will tend to get more. Those who focus upon the positive in life and attract it to them are called "lucky." I personally believe we can create our own luck. That is what's meant when it says in the Bible, "As a man thinketh, so is he."

> When asked the secret to great wealth, billionaire H.L. Hunt gave a simple four-step formula: 1. Decide on what it is that you want. 2. Decide what you are willing to give up to get it. 3. Set your priorities accordingly. 4. Be about it!

Whether you choose to believe in the law of attraction or not, it's interesting to note that many highly successful people do. This is one reason why rich people tend to associate with other rich people and why they get richer. Your thoughts are an energy that is both powerful and creative.

Some people believe the mind is like a magnet, and what we hold uppermost in our attention we attract to us. In music, this is called the principle of "sympathetic resonance." If you have two pianos in the same room and you hit a C note on one piano, you will find that the C string on the other piano starts vibrating at the same rate. In the same way you are always attracting people and circumstances that resonate with your predominant thoughts. Wouldn't it be good to attune your mind to notice how many opportunities there are to become wealthier? If you want to become rich and stay rich, you need to begin thinking of your-self as someone who deserves great wealth. You must begin by feeling rich within for it to manifest outwardly. As you begin to truly see yourself as a wealthy person, you will see your financial abundance grow.

> *"Some men see things as they are and ask, Why? I dream things that never were and ask, Why not?"*
> GEORGE BERNARD SHAW

Creating Wealth Consciousness

What we are going to do next will help you develop and install in your mind a wealth consciousness. This is about much more than attracting money— it's a change in your self-image to one of greater con-fidence and greater harmony so you begin to notice the abundance that surrounds you, and it will greatly enhance your experience of being alive.

I'd like to share with you the same techniques that I used myself to dramatically increase my personal financial wealth. I taught them to others, and they also increased their financial wealth. Now I'm going to share them with you.

Installing the Millionaire's Mind-set

When I first decided to make the shift from a poverty consciousness to one of wealth, I was constantly worrying about being poor or how not to be poor. I had a scruffy little checkbook that reflected my scruffy little finances at the time. When a bill came through the mail I'd worry about how I was going to pay it, and I'd feel poor inside. This continual focus on poverty kept me stuck in poor thinking and poor decision-making.

Once I'd made the decision to affirm wealth instead, I began to open my bills and vividly imagine that I had thousands in the bank, far more than I needed to pay the bill. You can imagine how good that feels. I was sending a new message to my unconscious. Some people try to get the same effect by saying affirmations like "I am wealthy, I am wealthy, I am wealthy," but if there is a belief in the unconscious about poverty, the affirmation is next to useless. It's not enough to hide your head in the sand and pretend—you have to actually create the feeling of wealth by vividly imagining yourself as wealthy over and over again.

Of course, you do have to pay your bills, but creating the feeling of wealth will make the process more enjoyable and send you on the road to greater abundance.

The mind is sensitive, so it's important to signal to yourself that "positive changes are happening." I changed banks and got a clean new checkbook to help me start to feel different. Then the real fun began.

I needed to get a strong sense of what greater wealth would be like, so I got an old bank statement, cut it up, removed the bit that said "overdrawn," rearranged the figures, and glued it back together showing thousands in credit. As soon as I'd finished, I burst out laughing. Somehow, even though I knew I'd made it up, actually holding it in my hands made it begin to feel more real. I focused on it several times every day.

Another technique I used was to practice writing out checks and withdrawal slips for hundreds of thousands of dollars until I felt comfortable doing it. By the time I was able to feel comfortable "depositing" and "spending" such large amounts, it was easy for me to see myself as a truly wealthy person.

To my surprise, within a few months the imaginary amount on my homemade bank statement had become a reality. Having that tangible piece of paper, the bank statement, had really helped.

So I searched for other ways to make my wealth consciousness tangible.

I decided to make a "wealth scrapbook," collecting pictures of things I wanted, places I wanted to visit, and people I wanted to meet. In order to make your own "wealth scrapbook," start collecting pictures of things you want, people you'd like to meet, places you'd like to go, and things you want to have. Anything you'd like to bring into your life, bring into your scrapbook.

Then, every time you look through your book, practice creating sensory-rich experiences of your goals. If it's a particular car, look into getting a test-drive so that afterward you can vividly imagine driving one, over and over again. If it's a beautiful house, imagine walking around it until you know every inch of it—the feeling of the carpet, the smell of the hallway, the texture of the furniture, and so on. It's very simple, but it does take regular practice. You are rehearsing being wealthy, and like a method actor, you need to totally get into the part.

One time, I went into a Mercedes showroom and sat in a car to get comfortable. I smelled the leather, went for a test-drive, and imagined it was my own. I took away a brochure to add to my scrapbook and imagined driving it every day. Pretty soon, my mind was so focused upon getting me one that I started to see Mercedes everywhere. Before long, a seeming coincidence brought a bargain deal my way, and I bought my first Mercedes.

A friend of mine got really into this type of creative visualization. He'd been practicing visualizing parking spaces, and amazingly it seemed to work. So he decided to go for bigger things.

Although he'd never been outside of England, he decided that he wanted to travel the world in style. Even though he didn't have much money, he collected some travel brochures, cut out the pictures of all the exotic places he wanted to go to, and stuck them in his scrapbook. Then, in order to make it real to himself, each Sunday for a month he packed his suitcase and went to the airport, even standing in line before finally turning around and going home.

When he arrived home, he'd watch a video of a program about traveling first class and spend time looking through his scrapbook at all the places he wanted to go. He really gave himself, his unconscious, that experience of traveling to and enjoying exotic locations. He focused on it for a month nonstop.

One day, with no warning, he was called into his boss's office and asked if he would like to become their international reporter. His boss explained it would mean traveling all over the world—first class. He could hardly believe it!

Most amazing of all, after a few months of travelling, he arrived at a small village in Switzerland where he began to get a feeling of déjà vu. It was only when he got back to England and checked in his scrapbook that he found it—he'd been staying in the exact same village he'd cut out and pasted into his scrapbook and ultimately his unconscious mind.

> "All the money in the world is spent on feeling good."
>
> RY COODER

Extraordinary as it may seem, I have witnessed so many such occurrences that I have become skeptical about the idea of "coincidences," and am willing to consider that although I don't know exactly how it works, our minds may actually have the ability to attract events, things, or people into our lives.

Money, Happiness, and You

Before we go any further, let me ask you a question:

What would having more money give you that you don't already have?

Whenever I ask this question on my seminars, people answer things like "happiness," "freedom," "security," or "power." However, money itself is not the source of any of these things. Each of these words represents a state you can generate within you, a neurochemical event in your body and mind. Let's face it—if money was *really* the key to happiness, freedom, security, or power, people like Kurt Cobain, Elvis Presley, Marilyn Monroe, and John Belushi would still be with us today.

Here's a corollary to the law of reversed effort:

If you want to get something in order to feel a certain way, feeling that way now will be the fastest way to get it.

Try the following technique to apply this principle to creating financial abundance!

ANCHOR YOURSELF TO WEALTH

1. Make a list of all the states and feelings you believe
   money will bring you.
   Examples: confident, happy, peaceful, generous, etc.

2. Choose the first state on your list. Remember a
   time when you really felt that way. Fully return
   to it now—see what you saw, hear what you
   heard, and feel how good you felt. (If you can't
   remember a time, imagine how much better your
   life would be if you felt that way now!)

3. Keep going through this memory. Make the
   colors brighter and richer, the sounds louder, and
   the feelings stronger.

4. As you feel these good feelings, squeeze the
   thumb and middle finger of one of your hands
   together and say the words "I am wealthy!" in
   your mind or out loud.

5. Repeat steps 2–3 with each emotional state on
   your list. Soon, just squeezing the thumb and
   middle finger together and repeating the phrase
   "I am wealthy!" will begin to bring back all those
   good feelings you associate with wealth.

This is your "wealth anchor." Use it any time you
are thinking about or wanting more money to condition yourself for success!

Success, Money, and Time

Another one of the fundamental aspects of the millionaire's mind-set is separating your ability to make money from the necessity of spending time to do it. Trading your time for money is the cornerstone of poverty consciousness. That's why you'll never meet a millionaire working for an hourly wage!

If you want to create massive financial abundance, it is necessary to first recognize that your ability to make money is intimately linked to your ability to add, create, and provide value, whether to a person, a project, a company, or an enterprise. In fact, I'll say it even more clearly:

Money is one of the rewards you get for adding value to the lives of others.

There are essentially four keys to making more money by adding more value:

1. Uniqueness
The more unique the value you provide, the more you will be able to exchange it for. While there are tens of thousands of actors in Hollywood, there are only about six at any one time who can reliably fill

seats, regardless of the movie they're in. That's why there are only about six actors in the world who are paid in excess of $20,000,000 a movie.

2. Scope
The more people you add value to, the more money you get to make. Whatever you might think of Bill Gates and Microsoft, their billions of dollars in net worth is largely accounted for by the millions of people whose lives are impacted daily by the development of Windows and its competitive operating systems.

3. Impact
The more of a difference you make in the lives of others, the more money you can demand in return. Why do most doctors get paid more than most teachers? Because most people value their health above their education.

4. Perception
There are many stories of people working tirelessly and anonymously behind the scenes to make a difference in the world. While it may be true that these unsung heroes are the real reason why the world works as well as it does, this does not mean that these people are destined to become rich. No matter

how much value you add to the world, it is only *perceived* value that can be exchanged for hard currency.

In the early 1970s, a record label in Britain was selling albums containing cover versions of contemporary songs. Although the records sold for less than a pound a copy, hardly anyone bought them and the record company was suffering.

A whizz kid joined the board and announced he wanted to more than double the price of the records. The other executives were shocked, but eventually agreed to his plan. Within a few weeks, the records were flying off the shelves. When the records didn't cost much people didn't value them. The record company was saved by redefining people's perception of the value of their product.

In simple terms, in order to create money, I believe you need to give something to the world that people will pay you for, preferably plenty. You might find it useful to ask yourself the following wealth-producing question:

What unique product or service would I like to provide that will be of massive value to the world?

Keeping Score with Money

It has been said many times that in the game of life, money is just a way of keeping score.

Now, if you're someone who has never balanced a checkbook or reconciled your accounts, this might seem a bit scary at first, but when you know where you are in relation to money, it becomes possible to measure your progress.

And as Michael LeBoeuf says in *The Greatest Management Principle in the World*,

What gets measured gets done.

You will need to get some paper, a calculator, and very possibly a sense of humor!

Wealth Measure Number One: Your Net Worth

Net worth is a traditional measure of wealth, and is reached by adding all your assets in one column and all your debits in the other.

Divide a piece of paper into two columns. On the left-hand side, write "Assets"; on the right, "Liabilities." In the Assets column, write down anything that you own and approximately what that thing would be worth if you sold it today.

In the Liabilities column, write down anything you still owe money for. This might include your home, your car, and any money you owe on credit cards or other outstanding loans.

The formula for determining net worth is simple:

Total Assets – Total Liabilities = Net Worth

Don't be discouraged if you find you have a negative net worth—the journey to wealth always begins exactly where you are!

Here's an example of how it might work:

ASSETS	LIABILITIES
House—150,000	Mortgage—100,000
Car—10,000	Car Loan—3,000
401(k)—35,000	School Loan—15,000
Money owed me— 3,500	Outstanding bills— 2500
Life Insurance cash value—15,000	Credit cards—4,500

Total assets = 213,500
Total liabilities= 125,000
213,500 - 125,000 = 88,500
Net worth = 88,500

Wealth Measure Number Two: The number of days forward you can live without earning any more money

To calculate your next "wealth score," simply take your typical monthly expenses and divide by 30. Let's call the answer your "daily rate." Then divide your net worth (how much you've got minus how much you owe) by your daily rate. The answer is the number of days forward you can live without earning any more money. As your earnings, savings and investments continue to grow, you can "keep score" by how many days you've added to your wealth score.

Example:

You have a net worth of $100,000 and monthly expenses of $5,000. $5,000 divided by 30 is $166.66, or $167. This is your daily rate. $100,000 divided by $167 is $598.8, or $599. This means that if you had to, you could maintain your current lifestyle without earning any more money for 599 days (about 1⅔ years).

Wealth Measure Number Three: The amount of money you wouldn't worry about losing

This one's more subjective, and easier to calculate. For example: twenty years ago, I lost five dollars and was nearly suicidal. Nowadays, if it's less than five hundred dollars, I don't worry about it. Using this scale, my wealth score has gone from about 5 to over 500. Partly, this is because I have more money. Partly, it's because I'm more confident in my ability to earn more money. Partly, I've just learned to relax. This is one of my favorite measures of wealth, because it's possible to increase it without earning any more money.

Wealth Measure Number Four: Your magic number for financial independence

This is one of the most useful money formulas you'll ever come across. It will help you to calculate your "magic number" for financial independence—the amount of money that, if you put it in the bank at an average (6–8 percent) rate of return, would allow you to make all your decisions independent of financial consideration.

1. Make a list of all the one-off purchases you would like to make in your lifetime and the approximate price—particularly any "big ticket" items.

Example:

House—$250,000
Cars—$50,000
A luxury holiday—$5,000
University education (x3)—$150,000
Miscellaneous fun—$45,000

2. Total up all the items—this is figure "A."

Example:

In our mathematically convenient example above, $500,000 would serve us nicely!

3. Decide on a comfortable annual "salary for life." (If in doubt, just double your existing salary!)

Example:

If you currently earn $25,000, figure that $50,000 a year for life would probably cover your ongoing needs and wants.

4. **Multiply that salary amount by 12 (approx. 8 percent return) or by 15 (approx. 6 percent return). This is the figure you would need to invest at a fairly conservative rate of return to "earn" your annual salary for life—we'll call it figure "B."**

Example:

Between $600,000 and $750,000

5. **Figure "A" + Figure "B" = Your Magic Number—the amount of money you would need to have in the bank in order to be utterly financially independent—i.e., able to make all your decisions independent of financial concern or consideration**

Example:

Magic Number = $1.25 million for financial
independence
(500,000 [A] + 750,000 [B])

The Ten Secrets of Abundance

Here are the ten best ideas I can give you on how
to start increasing your "wealth scores" today. Any
one of these will make an immediate difference to
your wealth consciousness. As you start using more
and more of them in your day-to-day life, you'll find
yourself on the fast track toward a wealthier life,
with the millionaire's mind. . . .

1. **Decide right now that you are responsible for
your financial abundance.**
Far too many people are scared to accept the responsibility of huge financial wealth. While it's true that
when you get more money, your financial pressures
don't get smaller, they get bigger—what most people
don't realize is that that's the fun of it!

As you accept the responsibility that comes with
playing the bigger money game, you become a more

capable person. The more substantial the challenges, the more substantial the rewards, not only financially, but spiritually and emotionally as well. And as you take responsibility for your own financial success, getting wealthier will seem less and less overwhelming and more like the pleasure it was always meant to be.

2. Save first, then spend only what you can truly afford.

In the same way as the real "secret" of losing weight is eating less and moving more, the real "secret" of gaining wealth is spending less and earning more. Create a plan today that will enable you to clear any outstanding debts and build your financial reservoir (see number 4!) as quickly as possible.

Consider taking the first 10 percent of your monthly income and immediately using it to pay down your debt and/or build your savings. As you take steps to reduce your debt and increase your net worth month by month, you'll quickly make the transition from trying to "keep your head above water" to starting to lay the foundations of wealth.

> *"The difference between poor people and rich people is easy. The poor spend their money and then save what's left over; the rich save their money and then spend what's left over."*
>
> JIM ROHN

3. Study wealthy people.

One of the quickest ways to become wealthy is to spend time with those people who have already achieved wealth. Remember, wealth is more than financial abundance—many people have become millionaires only to discover that along the way they lost something far more important—their own respect and sense of self.

> "If you want to learn about money, learn from somebody who has a lot of it."
>
> CHARLES GIVENS

Take some time to research and discover your own "heroes of wealth"— those people who've found a way to create massive financial abundance without sacrificing their lives or their souls along the way. Find out what they are doing that you aren't. Seek to understand how they think and behave toward money and wealth. If possible, contact them and ask for advice. Not only does asking make other people aware of who you are, it also lets them know that you are taking your pursuit of wealth seriously. While not everyone will offer to help, it's been my experience that as long as you are polite and respectful, many wealthy people are grateful for the opportunity to be of service.

4. Build your financial reservoir.

The more money you have in the bank, the less frightening it is to experiment with new and different ways of making money. This is why the most powerful investment you can make is to build your financial reservoir—a savings account with between three months' and two years' salary in it.

In Dr. Richard Carlson's book *Don't Worry, Make Money*, he tells the story of two men who were both offered the same job with a new company in the 1970s. The offer was for very low pay, but a large piece of stock. The man who was living from paycheck to paycheck thought it was too risky and passed; the one who had a financial reservoir took the offer. The company was Microsoft and, needless to say, within a few years the man who took the risk had amassed a huge fortune.

The moral of the story is that in most cases, creating abundance usually involves some risk, and nothing makes risk more tolerable than having money in the bank. As author Stuart Wilde says, "The trick to money is having some."

5. The 80/20 rule

Once you figure out what is most important to you, you can prioritize your life accordingly. Nineteenth-century economist Vilfrido Pareto was the first to point out that approximately 80 percent of the world's wealth was concentrated in the hands of only 20 percent of the world's population.

The 80/20 rule holds true in most areas of life—80 percent of your results will tend to come from 20 percent of your efforts; 80 percent of your wealth will come from 20 percent of your clients or customers. By identifying and concentrating on that all-important 20 percent, we can continually refocus our priorities with a laser-like intensity.

6. **Get in touch with your passion every day.**

I remember that years ago, when I first got interested in hypnosis, one of the old stage performers I was learning from was also a salesman. This wasn't just his job—it was his passion. I never saw him go more than a few hours without selling something to someone. We'd be at a restaurant and he'd strike up a conversation with a person at another table. Before long, he'd find out all about their needs and offer to sell them exactly what they wanted. Most of the time, he didn't even have what he'd just sold— he'd have to go out and buy it himself in order to turn around and deliver it to the person who'd just bought it from him. He simply loved the thrill of persuading people.

When I asked him what he thought his secret was, he said:

"Excitement and passion are contagious. When you get truly passionate about what you want to do, others will find themselves drawn to you."

7. Charge what you are truly worth.

Some people are frightened to charge what they are really worth, because they fear they will lose their clients. But in my own experience, every time I have raised my fees I've found myself attracting more and better clients and losing only those people I wasn't particularly enjoying working with anyway.

Here's a simple formula for working out what your time is worth, no matter how much or little you may earn:

1. Write down the amount of money you expect to earn this year.

2. Erase or cross out the last three numbers.

3. Divide by two. This is what an hour of your time is worth, based on an average working week.

Example: Annual earnings = $30,000. Less last three numbers = $30. Divided by two = $15. Your hourly "wage" is $15.

Just for today, imagine your hourly wage has doubled. If you were being paid twice as much per hour for what you do, what would you do differently?

If you want to charge what you're truly worth, start doing it differently today!

8. **Regularly practice the *Change Your Life in 7 Days* techniques.**

For most people, opportunities to become wealthier present themselves every day without ever being noticed. By practicing the techniques and listening to the mind-programming CD, you are conditioning yourself to focus on wealth. Very few multimillionaires get to be rich by accident. Financial success is simply a matter of maintaining your focus on wealth and consistently practicing the actions that lead to abundance.

> *"Life is so simple, really. Think through what people want, invite them to get it from you, and when they show up, bill 'em!"*
>
> STUART WILDE

Take some time each day to walk around as if you already have everything you want. Create a sensory-rich experience of what you want so your unconscious mind gets a clear idea. Ask yourself empowering questions. Create a wealth scrapbook and imagine what it would be like living the life of your dreams. See what you'll see, hear, and feel. Do it as often as you can every day.

You may not get instant results, but you will attract to you in one way or another whatever you think about most. Use your favorite techniques daily to condition yourself for success!

9. Celebrate your life, starting today!

One of the single most important things you can do to cement your wealth consciousness is to make a practice of reflecting on all the good things in your life as you drift off to sleep each night. As you say thank you to life, God, the universe, or whatever you feel most comfortable with and connected to, you are cultivating "an attitude of gratitude."

> "Today's gratitude buys tomorrow's happiness."
> MICHAEL MCMILLIAN

An attitude of gratitude is the exact opposite of a poverty consciousness. When you start to regularly think of all the good things you have and of how fortunate you are to have them, you are sending a strong message of abundance to your unconscious that will create a steady flow of financial abundance.

10. Keep going.

There is a story that in ancient Tibet, all the monks were gathered together once every hundred

> "Never give in. Never give in. Never, never, never, never—in nothing, great or small, large or petty— never give in, except to convictions of honor and good sense. Never yield to force. Never yield to the apparently overwhelming might of the enemy."
>
> SIR WINSTON CHURCHILL

years and given an opportunity for guaranteed enlightenment—all they had to do was walk through the "Room of a Thousand Demons" and come out alive. The Room of a Thousand Demons was a pitch-black room filled with a thousand demons who would appear to you in the guise of your biggest and worst fears: spiders, snakes, sheer precipices—whatever they sensed would fill your heart with terror. The only rules were that once you entered no one could come in and rescue you, and it was impossible to leave by the door you went in. For those few brave souls who dared to face their fears in pursuit of happiness, success, and enlightenment, there was one crucial piece of advice:

No matter what you think you see, hear, think, or feel, keep your feet moving. If you keep your feet moving, you will eventually get to where it is you want to go!

Perhaps my favorite quote on the power of persistence comes from president Calvin Coolidge:

*"Nothing in the world can take the place
of persistence. Talent will not; nothing
is more common than unsuccessful
men with talent. Genius will not;
unrewarded genius is almost a proverb.
Education will not; the world is full
of educated derelicts. Persistence and
determination alone are omnipotent."*

In Conclusion

Finally, I want you to remember that real wealth is not measured by money alone. Start today. Create a plan for financial abundance and start moving forward. Make the changes you need to make, both at the level of your consciousness and in action. After you have begun to enjoy more of the success that you desire, you will look back and be thankful that you did!

Until tomorrow,

Paul McKenna

P.S. Tomorrow is the last day of your seven-day program, and we'll be dealing with an appropriate topic as this program draws to a close—the secrets of living happily ever after. . . .

DAY SEVEN

Happily Ever After

Live the secrets of life-long happiness—now!

BEFORE YOU BEGIN TODAY:

- Listen to the mind-programming session on the CD.

- Take a few minutes to go through the Reprogramming Your Self-image for Success exercise on page 41.

- Review your purpose, values, and big dream from day four.

- Use your wealth anchor and do a one-minute wealth visualization:

Imagine you already have all the good feelings you know that being wealthy will bring you. All the happiness, all the confidence and all the love you could ever hope for is there inside you. . . .

Now imagine yourself going through your day. How do you treat people? How do they treat you? What are you especially proud of about today? What do you love doing? What do you do exceptionally well?

What value have you added today? How could you add even more? Who else could you impact with your work? How about with your life?

Finally, imagine yourself listening to the evening programming session before drifting off into a deep, relaxing sleep, knowing you have programmed yourself to have a fantastically successful day!

ONE DAY, A WEALTHY BUSINESSMAN hired a fishing boat to take him out to sea for a day of relaxation. The sun was shining, and the wealthy man took a liking to the happy young fisherman who guided the fishing boat through the waters of the harbor.

"Young man," said the wealthy businessman. "I can teach you the secrets of success, if you'll only listen carefully."

"OK," said the young fisherman, smiling as he cleaned the morning's catch.

Although he was a bit taken aback by the young man's casual manner, the businessman began his lesson.

"First off, double your prices. You run a good, clean boat and you know where the fish are plentiful."

"Why would I want to do that?" replied the young fisherman, distracted by watching a small crab playing in the waves by the shore.

The businessman could feel the irritation rising as he replied.

"Because then you will be able to buy a second boat, and a third, and you will be able to take on more tourists and catch more fish. If you work hard, you will earn enough to buy a whole fleet of boats."

"But why would I want to do that?" the young fisherman asked as he rolled over onto his back to soak up the last gentle rays of the afternoon sun.

By now, the businessman was furious.

"Because then you will become rich, and you can hire people to do your work for you while you spend your days fishing and relaxing in the sun!"

"Ah," the young fisherman said, nodding sagely. "That sounds wonderful!"

Two Kinds of Happiness

I believe that there are two kinds of happiness in the world. The one most of us think of is simply feeling wonderful in your body. The other, more subtle form of happiness is a state of being in perfect harmony with life, the universe, and everything. This is the state that psychologists call "flow," musicians call "the groove," and athletes call "the zone." Today, you will be learning how to take responsibility for your own happiness, and the secrets of bringing more of both kinds of happiness

> *"I have come to understand that life is best to be lived and not to be conceptualized. I am happy because I am growing daily and I am honestly not knowing where the limit lies."*
>
> BRUCE LEE

In the West, our culture emphasizes the pursuit of happiness through external means. Most people would complete the sentence, "I'll be happy when ____" with externals like, "When I've made a million dollars." "When I'm married to the person of my dreams." "When I find a job," etc. We are told from a very early age that these are the things that will make us happy, but a quick glance at the news each day reveals clearly that having "the good things in life" can only be part of the story.

In the East, traditional culture emphasizes acceptance of the conditions of existence, positing the idea that happiness is found within. My own experience suggests that while the eastern ideal of happiness coming from within is more accurate, having grown up in the West it's a lot easier to be happy when your life doesn't suck. Personally, I believe it's good to have a balance.

HERE IS TODAY'S KEY LESSON:

Happiness is not a result—it's a state of mind and body.

The good news is that you already know how easy it is to create states, and you can learn to experience that state we call happiness much more often than you do right now.

Think a little more deeply now—what does happiness feel like in your body?

For some, it's a warm, peaceful, glowing feeling. Other people describe it as a kind of delightful sense of inner satisfaction. While I don't know precisely what happiness feels like for you, I do know that if you began to have that feeling that you call happiness in your body right now, you could identify it in an instant.

When Is It Not OK to Be Happy?

Many people put obstacles in the way of feeling happiness. While some people are still waiting for things outside them to "make them happy," others are concerned about feeling happiness inappropriately.

I was leading a seminar on creating happiness when a participant stood up with tears in his eyes.

"My daughter just died," the man said. "Are you saying I'm supposed to be happy about that?"

First I said: "It's only right, only natural that you are sad about the death of your daughter. You feel sad because she meant so much to you, but would she want you to feel sad forever?" As he thought about it I asked him to reflect on all the good times he had with his daughter—all the love that he shared with her and all the experiences they had enjoyed together. When I could see that he was really connected to his experience, I asked him how he thought she would want him to feel.

He paused for a moment, then a smile began to shine across his face beneath the tears. When he finally spoke, we could all hear the love in his heart as he said simply, "She would want me to be happy."

We all have our own "rules" for when happiness is an inappropriate response to what is going on around us. The important thing to remember is that happiness is first and foremost a choice. As Abraham Lincoln once said: "Most people are about as happy as they make up their minds to be."

The Science of Happiness

A few years ago I heard about a medical doctor in New York who helped drug addicts overcome their addictions by putting them into a trance and teaching their bodies to create the response to the drug. Once they learned the technique, they were able to get "high" naturally. Since they now realized it was their body that was making them feel so good and not the drugs, it became progressively easier for them to wean themselves off their chemical dependency.

Here's how it works.

Any drug you've ever taken created a specific neurochemical response in your body. This response is the source of the "high." In other words, it's not what the drug does that makes you feel a particular way, it's what your body does *in response* to the drug that gives you the feeling.

While I was very impressed with the research behind the doctor's work, what particularly interested me was the idea of creating "happiness on demand"—that is, the process of teaching the mind to get the body to create the chemicals inside that lead to good feelings where and when we want them.

For decades, researchers had been trying to find out what it was that allowed the drug opium to have its euphoric effects. When Dr. Candace Pert was still only a graduate student, she discovered what are called the "opiate receptors," not just in the brain, but in every single cell in the body.

She found these receptors were particularly in tune with one special kind of chemical messenger, called "endogenous morphine," or more commonly "endorphin." Endorphins are your body's natural opiates, the neurotransmitters that control pain and create pleasure. There are happy chemicals inside you!

You have a natural endorphin release when you do physical exercise, make love, laugh a lot, or relax deeply. You know how it feels on a cold winter's day to sli-i-i-ide into a hot bath and get that feeling of gentle warmth? Or when you eat your favorite food, how good it feels? That's the feeling of endorphins at play in your body.

But endorphins are more than just the source of good feelings in your body. Because endorphins are neurotransmitters, they create more connections in the brain, so every time you experience an endorphin release, it actually makes you more intelligent. And every cell in your body has receptors for endorphins.

How great a design feature is that? Not only can every cell in our body experience happiness but the more often we choose to be happy, the more intelligent we become!

The way that your brain and body communicate to let you know that it's time to feel good is cell to cell. A chemical message trips off at one cell, takes on the shape for the endorphin and sets up a vibration, and the cells next door go, "Wow—there's something coooool going on!" and they start resonating in the same way. Then, the message spreads from cell to cell, like a wave of pleasure. Now, when you experience a wave of pleasure, you feel so good because every cell in your body is sharing that state.

When I heard about the doctor who was helping drug addicts to overcome their addiction by getting naturally high using hypnosis, I started experimenting to see if I could get people to have endorphin releases using imagination exercises. Not only were many of them able instantly to experience those great feelings but also it was without any formal hypnotic induction, just using a simple imagination technique.

People I tried it with suddenly found they felt fantastic! I would simply ask them to remember times in the past when their endorphins were flowing, then to turn up the brightness and color of those happy memories and keep going through them again and again until some people were smiling with delight while they nearly fell off their chairs laughing.

Since then I have taught thousands of people how to give themselves an instant endorphin release. Recently a psychiatrist wrote to me and explained how he'd been using the technique with his patients who suffered from depression and how much it had helped them.

Let's get happy right now. . . .

INSTANT ENDORPHIN RELEASE

1. Remember a time when you felt totally happy and at peace. Return fully to that time now, seeing what you saw, hearing what you heard, and feeling how good you felt. (If you can't remember a specific time, just imagine how much better your life would be if you were totally happy and peaceful right now—if you had all the peace, love, and contentment you could ever want.)

2. Now make the colors brighter and richer, the sounds louder, and allow your feelings of happiness to intensify.

3. Notice where that feeling of happiness is strongest in your body. Give this feeling of happiness a color, and move that color up to the top of your head and down to the tip of your toes. Double the brightness. Double it again!

4. You can visualize the endorphins like little dolphins at play in your bloodstream, happily swimming from cell to cell. Or feel the flow of endorphins like a river of golden honey throughout your body.

5. Repeat steps 2–4 at least five more times. Vividly imagine in detail that event where you are happy, again and again. You can use the same happy experience or add in new ones each time.

When I first discovered this I thought, Fantastic—I'll just feel great all the time! However, as with any emotional state, it is important to have a sense of context. When you're crossing the road, it is not the wisest idea to be buzzed out of your mind on endorphins. When you're driving, you want to have your wits about you while negotiating the traffic.

However, whenever it's appropriate to feel wonderful, why not make use of this great natural technique?

Designer Happiness

Professor Mihaly Csikszentmihalyi from the University of Chicago has spent more than thirty years studying happiness. Because he couldn't get funding to research happiness directly (it wasn't considered a sufficiently serious subject for scientific study), his studies focus on what he calls "optimal experiences," or "flow."

As a result of his research, he has identified eight characteristics that are invariably present during optimal experience—that is, the experience of happiness, enjoyment, and fulfillment in the moment of doing whatever it is you are doing.

Each of the characteristics serves as a potential

happiness trigger—a way of turning an ordinary situation into an optimal, enjoyable flow experience. As you read them now you may well have ideas about where you can create more opportunities for them in your life and begin to feel the flow state start happening.

The eight happiness triggers are:

1. Clear goals

Having a clear goal, purpose, or intention acts as a sort of an organizing principle for our attention, filtering our experience down from a world of infinite possibilities to a selective collection of experiences that allow us to focus, feel in control, "make sense" of what is happening to us, and respond deliberately.

Therefore, the simplest way to transform any task into a potential flow experience is to set for ourselves an intention, purpose, or goal in relation to that task.

In cases where the task is mundane, repetitive, or simply not interesting to us, our intention need not be directly related to the actual task. For instance, living the intention of "being fully present" can turn a "boring" drive into a Zen meditation; living the intention of "performing with energy, enthusiasm, and as if it's the most important thing in the world" can turn washing the dishes into an enjoyable activity.

2. Immediate feedback

Do you remember as a child playing the "warmer/colder" game? The closer you got to your "goal," the hidden object you were seeking, the "warmer" you were; the further away, the "colder."

The reason this game is so popular cross-culturally is that the human brain is designed as a cybernetic mechanism—that is, it thrives on having a clear goal and making constant adjustments in pursuit of that goal, just like a heat-seeking missile. However, in order to function at its full capacity, we must give it continual feedback as to whether we are on track.

3. Ability to concentrate on the task at hand

Often geniuses are characterized as being like plate-spinners in a circus, able to keep many different tasks going at any one time. And yet, one trait that consistently comes up in the research into creativity and flow is that both are most likely to occur when you are focused on only one thing at a time. In fact, when asked how he had come up with the theory of gravity, Sir Isaac Newton is reputed to have said, "You would have come up with it too if you had spent all your time thinking of nothing else!"

4. The possibility of successful completion

One of the key factors in successful recovery from any illness is hope—the belief that things can get better, given time. Similarly if we want to turn an ordinary experience into a "flow" experience, we must generate feel-

> "Confidence is preparation in action."
> RON HOWARD

ings of hope or possibility that we will be able to successfully complete the project or task at hand.

Our probability of success goes up any time we choose attitudes and actions that are both within our control and also increase the likelihood of getting what we want either now or in the future. Things like preparation, daily action, and inviting others to participate in our goals and dreams not only make our success more likely in reality, they make it more believable in our minds and hearts, increasing our will to succeed by making the path to success more and more apparent.

5. Total involvement

Rock climbing is something that always puzzled me. Why would anyone want to do that? Why would anyone aspire to the same skill level that a small lizard demonstrates? There doesn't appear to be any gain in it. Even more confusing, climbs aren't rated by your ability to get to the top, but rather by the route you choose to take. Fellow climbers are far more impressed by an interesting journey than by reaching the destination.

And that's part of its appeal: climbing for climbing's sake. Many climbers report that when they've reached the top of a rock, after the relief has subsided, there's a desire for it to go on and on.

One climbing instructor I knew created an interesting "entrance exam" for his advanced climbing course. He assigned all the potential students an extremely difficult climb. The instructor told the aspiring students that he would make his decision when they reached the top, then secreted himself behind a rock partway up at what is known as a "false summit"—i.e. something that appears to be the top of the mountain but isn't.

When the students reached the false summit, he would watch their faces as they realized that rather than being done, they were still only partway to the top. Those who appeared disappointed were politely refused entry to the advanced group, but those whose eyes widened in excitement at the prospect of more climbing ahead were welcomed with open arms.

According to Csikszentmihalyi, most optimal experience is the result of this kind of "teleological" activity—that is, activity that is intrinsically satisfying as opposed to goal-orientated. When we do things not because we believe it will necessarily make us look good or make us money but for the sheer love of doing the thing, we increase the likelihood of experiencing flow.

6. Loss of self-consciousness

One of the things that people often report after being hypnotized at my shows is that it allows them, sometimes for the first time in their adult lives, to feel totally unself-conscious. While we all live in this state as small children, by the time we're about five we have already begun to judge ourselves through the eyes of the people around us. When we are able to become completely absorbed in a flow experience, we return to that pleasant state where what we are doing and experiencing becomes far more interesting than what other people might be thinking.

7. A sense of control

A study reported in the *New York Times* points out the significance of a sense of control in our lives.

The feeling of being in control, of having a say in what happens in one's life, has far-reaching consequences for physical and mental health. . . . Increasing the sense of control among men and women living in nursing homes made them happier, increased their alertness and—perhaps most dramatically—lowered their mortality rate, over a period of 18 months, by 50 percent.

The increased control came from simple changes, such as allowing the nursing-home residents to decide what they would have for meals, when the phone would ring in their rooms, and how the furniture would be arranged.

> "Put your hand on a hot stove for a minute, and it seems like an hour. Sit with a pretty girl for an hour, and it seems like a minute. That's relativity."
>
> ALBERT EINSTEIN

By taking control over even the simplest elements of our environment (where we are sitting, how things are arranged on our desk, or even what we are looking at when we daydream), we increase the likelihood of experiencing happiness in our everyday lives.

8. Time distortion (i.e., minutes becoming hours and/or hours feeling like minutes)

Have you noticed when you are doing some things time seems to move really slowly or really quickly? Here are some of my favorite time-distorting activities:

- **Sports that test your ability**

- Reading a book that gives illumination

- When drawing, correctly portraying perspective, light, and shade

- Driving on difficult terrain

- Dancing, hearing the beat and melody of a song and moving in an expressive way to it

- Thinking, reasoning through the strands of a problem, and arranging them in consciousness

- Noticing the subtle differences in taste of exotic foods

> *"Enjoyment appears at the boundary between boredom and anxiety, when the challenges are just balanced with the person's capacity to act."*
>
> MIHALY CSIKSZENTMIHALYI

Balancing Challenge and Mastery

While each one of these eight characteristics is important, perhaps the most useful one, if we want to design out own optimal experiences, is a ninth "meta-characteristic":

We tend to experience flow when there is a balance between our perception of the challenge we are facing and our perception of our ability to meet that challenge.

Fortunately, most of us have at least occasionally experienced the calm, focused energy that comes with performing in the flow zone, when we feel up to the challenges we are faced with.

Life, at its best, is a constant shuttle between mastery and challenge, a continual process of stretching and consolidating our gains and learning.

So how do we design and adjust our experience to ensure we have the highest possible chance of both enjoying an activity and performing at our best?

The key is in the word "perception"—that is, by adjusting our perceptions (of the challenges we face and of our ability to meet those challenges), we can literally re-create our experience for optimal performance.

Transforming Fear into Flow

Think of a situation, project, or activity that totally freaks you out—that you feel you should or must or even want to participate in but which is so far out of your league that you know you're bound to fail. This can be a business activity (quadrupling your sales volume in the next month) or a personal one (asking that person of your dreams out on a date).

BONUS TIP

It would appear that not all balance is created equally. Research shows that people are more likely to describe their experience and performance levels as "optimal" when both the challenge and skill are balanced at a high level (e.g., brain surgery) than at a low level (e.g., learning to use chopsticks).

Here are two simple strategies that will help you turn your feelings of panic or being overwhelmed into the focus of flow . . .

1. Lowering your sights

While conventional wisdom tells us to shoot for the stars, happiness research points out that lowering your sights and focusing on a target that you know you can hit can quickly turn even the most daunting challenge into a fun adventure. When Richard Bandler went to transform the US Army pistol-shooting program, one of the first things he did was cut the distance to the target in half. As people's confidence and skill increased, the targets were gradually returned to the original distance. The result—a vastly increased success rate in less than half the original training time.

> *Example: Quadrupling my sales volume*
> *"I lower my sights and set myself a smaller*
> *target—doubling my sales volume. No,*
> *still too scary. What if I try to increase my*
> *volume by one in the next week? Doesn't*
> *feel within my control. I know—I'll make*
> *twenty more calls a day than I did last*
> *month! That puts me firmly into flow."*

2. Focus on past success

If you've gotten this far in life, chances are you've done more than a few things right. When you start to focus on what you do that's working, your perception of your ability increases, and along with it you increase the possibility of flow.

> *Example: Asking dream lover out on a date*
> *"Hmmm . . . I've actually dated before.*
> *And some of them have even gone well!*
> *And remember that time that _____ said*
> *yes, which really surprised me? And that*
> *other time? And that other time? OK,*
> *my heart's still pumping, but it's turned*

into excitement—I'm still pumped up but it feels like a positive challenge."

ASK YOURSELF, "WHAT CAN I DO NOW?"

Background Happiness

Some psychologists believe in what they call "background stress." In other words, even though someone might be doing something enjoyable, there's still hidden worry lurking somewhere "back there." But rather than "background stress," I think it's a much better idea to have "background happiness": a kind of all-pervading feeling in the back of your mind that life is good, that your unconscious does everything it can to help you and all problems can be resolved in a healthy, life-enhancing way.

Can you learn how to do it? Absolutely. There are thousands and thousands of people walking around experiencing background happiness and flow in all areas of their lives, much to the annoyance of psychologists and therapists who continue to "prove" the impossibility of doing it.

In the past, many people have worked hard to

> *"The secret of being happy is not doing what one likes, but liking what one does."*
>
> J. M. BARRIE

create "flow" in their lives. However, there is an easy way to do it.

Whenever you've experienced flow in the past your unconscious mind has made a record of the psychological and physiological aspects of that optimum experience. This is because flow is a neurophysiological state: in other words, it is a set of electrical impulses in your brain and chemical changes in your body. Your mind and body have a multisensory recording of exactly how you make flow happen, of how you make that state.

So what we're going to do is get your unconscious mind to go on a search and find all the times in the past when you've experienced flow, then make a record of the state so that you can begin to trigger it for yourself more and more.

After a while almost anything you do can become effortless and joyous. You'll be doing something and you won't know why you feel so good, or why you are so harmoniously involved with what you are doing, and it will happen more and more.

One of the best ways to reaccess flow is by remembering a time when you were in the zone, in flow. Remember that the human nervous system cannot tell the difference between a real and a vividly imagined experience. All you need to do is remember a time you were in flow and amplify it. If you do this each day, it will program your mind and body to take you into the zone more and more, able to say the right things in just the right way at the right time, easily thinking of the perfect thing to do, gliding through your days with an amazing sense of satisfaction.

OK, let's do it now. . . .

STEPPING INTO THE ZONE

1. Make yourself comfortable, relax, and close your eyes.

2. Now remember times when you have been in states of flow, seeing what you saw, hearing what you heard, feeling how good you felt. This starts re-creating the flow state within you. . . .

3. Now amplify it: make the pictures bigger, brighter, bolder, the sounds louder, the feelings stronger, and anchor the state by squeezing your thumb and middle finger together (or any other self-anchor you want to use).

4. Now do it again, see what you saw, hear what you heard, feel how good you felt.

5. Now find another time when you experienced flow and go through the procedure all over again, seeing what you saw, hearing what you heard, feeling how good you felt, until you only have to squeeze your fingers together to feel yourself go into the flow state.

Ask your unconscious mind to trigger that flow state throughout the day. As you begin to find yourself experiencing flow more and more of the time, the neural pathways in your brain that create flow and background happiness become stronger and stronger until you hardwire yourself to be in flow all the time.

The Problem with Pleasure

A number of people have come to me over the years suffering from what I can only describe as "an excess of pleasure." I like to share with them a distinction between pleasure and what I will call "satisfaction"—i.e., between those things that feel good in the moment and those things that we feel good about afterward.

Here's the distinction in a nutshell:

Pleasures give the body pleasant sensations; satisfactions gratify the soul.

Does this mean pleasure is bad?

Not at all. But the problem with pleasure is that it feels so darn good, we can be easily tempted to put it at the top of our priority list as we pursue the good life at all costs. But the good life is largely devoid of the satisfactions that come when we pit ourselves against a worthy challenge. Perhaps this is why Sir Richard Branson continues to risk life and limb in a helium balloon—because he recognizes that too much of the so-called good life can be bad for you.

In fact, pleasure pursued for its own sake actually seems to get in the way of happiness. A lizard will starve to death if you try to hand-feed it, yet it will thrive when allowed to hunt its own food; an ear of corn will rot on the stalk if not challenged by wind and rain. And if you want to be happy, you need to take on a worthy challenge—even if that's the last thing you feel you want!

So how do we create a happier, more satisfying life?

1. Allow more pleasure into your life.

> "Every heart that has beat strongly and cheerfully has left a hopeful impulse behind it in the world, and bettered the tradition of mankind."
>
> ROBERT LOUIS STEVENSON

This may seem to go against everything I have been saying, but, for most of us, our lust for pleasure is tied in to the appeal of forbidden fruit. In fact, the word in our society most commonly paired with pleasure is "guilty." By making it OK to take time out to listen to the rain while taking a warm, candlelit bath (or watching football while drinking a beer!), we can stop spending so much time policing ourselves and begin taking more time to challenge ourselves.

2. Discover your strengths and begin to put them to work.

We tend to feel our best when we are doing our best,

and we can only do our best when we are doing what we do best—that is, playing to our strengths. While conventional wisdom encourages us to develop our weaknesses, research into success and fulfillment points out that when we play to our strengths and manage our weakness, we not only perform better but we get more satisfaction from our performance.

To identify your strengths, employ what management consultants call "360-degree feedback"—that is, ask people in every area of your life what they consider your strengths to be until you can clearly identify the common characteristics and standards.

3. Do at least one difficult thing each day.

When Mihaly Csikszentmihalyi completed his initial studies into "Flow and the Psychology of Optimal Experience," he was asked by a reporter to summarize the findings of what was a 2000-page document. After thinking for a moment, Csikszentmihalyi said:

*"Every day, the happy person does
at least one difficult thing."*

While it may seem odd to conclude a lesson in happiness by talking about deliberately seeking out difficulties, it is a lesson that life itself continually attempts to teach us.

Lillian Gilbreth, one of the most extraordinary women of the twentieth century and an early pioneer in the field of productivity, was asked what kept her so alive and vital into her seventies. She replied, "Every morning I ask God to give me a day filled with challenges and difficulties. Every evening I give thanks, as he always answers my morning prayer."

When seeking out worthy challenges in your own life, bear in mind that optimal experience tends to live at the balancing point at the outer edge of your abilities—when you're fully engaged but not overwhelmed by the challenge.

Congratulations, you're almost done! In the concluding chapter, I'll share with you some ideas on how to maintain and develop the changes that have been occurring over the last seven days.

Until then,

Paul McKenna

CONCLUSION

Changing Your Life, One
Week at a Time

It was registration day at the university, and the young man was preparing to continue the adventure in learning that had been going on so long it seemed to have no beginning and no end. Lost in thought, his mind racing with possibilities for what lay ahead, he barely noticed the old man in front of him until he bumped straight into him.

"I'm sorry, Professor," the young man said, embarrassed.

"Oh, I'm not a professor," the old man replied. "I'm a new student, just like you."

"But how old are you?" the young man said in shock.

"I'm seventy-three," the old man said with a twinkle in his eye.

"And what are you studying?" the young man continued.

"Medicine—I've always wanted to be a doctor, and now . . ." The old man paused as if remembering something from a long time ago. "Now, I'm finally ready to follow my dreams!"

The young man seemed quite shocked. "No disrespect, sir, but to become a doctor will take at least seven years. In seven years, you'll be eighty years old!"

The old man put his hand on the young man's shoulder and looked him straight in the eyes.

"God willing," the old man said, smiling, "I'll be eighty years old whether I follow my dreams or not."

The Power of Suggestion

In my hypnotic shows, I often offer the people on stage a post-hypnotic suggestion. Long after they think their part in the show is over, every time I say a key word or phrase they will begin to enact the behavior I have suggested to them.

Throughout this book, I have been giving suggestions for how you cannot only change your life but keep the change over the weeks, months, and years ahead. Some of these suggestions were direct—that is, you will have noticed my suggesting them as you read. However, others were indirect—embedded into the text in order to send them directly into your unconscious mind and designed to be triggered by the natural occurrences that happen in everyone's life.

Please know this:

Every single one of those suggestions will assist you in creating the life of your dreams, including the ones you are not even aware of yet. . . .

In order to facilitate and reinforce your ongoing success, I have created the following daily success workout. This is the same routine I use every morning to set myself up for a wonderful day. I suggest that for the next week or so, you follow this routine exactly as I have designed it for you. As you become more familiar with the techniques in the book, you can begin to substitute other exercises for the ones written here. By making time in your day to program your mind with positive suggestions, your energy and motivation will increase, and you will become happier, stronger, and more creative as your life continues to get even better. . . .

YOUR DAILY SUCCESS WORKOUT

1. Begin by taking three deep breaths. Each time you breathe in, feel any areas of tension and stress in your body. Each time you breathe out, feel yourself letting go and relaxing into a lovely, peaceful state.

2. Imagine the qualities of your authentic self. See yourself going through your day as your authentic self. Do this several times until it becomes easy to imagine.

3. Now, review your top five values. Take a moment to really feel each one, and once again guide your mind through the day ahead. Each time you do this, you are programming yourself to have a wonderful day!

4. Use the inner smile to activate your endorphin response. Smile into every area of yourself and keep feeling better and better and better.

5. Review your big dream. Ask your mind to guide you in thought, word, and action to do and say exactly the right things to make your dreams come true for the highest good of all concerned.

6. What are you most grateful for in your life? Spend at least one minute focused on all the good things you already have and everything that's right with your world.

7. Finish by taking three more deep breaths. This time, allow each breath in to fill you with energy and each breath out to energize you even more.

With practice, you will find you can complete this routine in as little as five minutes. However, I recommend that whenever possible, you take at least fifteen minutes to really set yourself up for the day. As Mahatma Gandhi once said in the midst of his campaign to create a free and self-governing India:

"I have so much to do today I will need to meditate twice as long!"

How Good Can it Get?

Finally, as we reach the end of the book, I'd like to talk about the future. You may remember I started this book by talking about how we live in a truly exciting time in our planet's history. These days there is more information to absorb, more to learn, and more opportunities than ever before.

> *"The illiterate of the twenty-first century will not be those who cannot read and write, but those who cannot learn, unlearn, and relearn."*
>
> ALVIN TOFFLER

As the pace of change gets quicker and quicker, the creative technology we have now is able to constantly upgrade and improve itself. A hundred and fifty years ago the telegraph first made it possible to send messages quickly over great distances. Within thirty years, the telephone had arrived, quickly followed by voice recording, radio, television, fax, and now e-mail.

We can now communicate across the planet in an instant. Something happens on one side of the world and we can watch it on our televisions, read about it on the Web, and communicate about it on the Internet, all sharing the experience simultaneously. The eyes and ears of our telecommunications network are becoming the eyes and ears of humanity.

More than ever, the mind is now the dominant creative force on this planet. Our thoughts are more powerful than they have ever been, and with the exponential enhancements in technology we are likely to see some amazing changes in the near future.

Some scientists believe that within the next few years we will have a cure for cancer, drugs to permanently increase intelligence, cryogenic preservation, and genetic control of ageing. Virtual reality, genetic reprogramming, and developments in nanotechnology will offer benefits we cannot even imagine, as today's science fiction becomes the template for tomorrow's science fact. We stand, many of us unknowingly, on the edge of an amazing leap in humanity's evolution.

To make this leap, we need a radical shift in our values. Rather than continually looking for fulfillment in the outside world, which has made us overly competitive and selfish, we need to begin to find more contentment within. I believe that a new age of "psycho-technology" is upon us, and the kind of techniques we've been using in this book will become what more and more people turn to in order to help bring about positive changes at every level of society.

These days, a country's wealth is no longer gauged by its physical resources. Instead, it is ideas and their implementation that create wealth. The real source of wealth is in our minds, and those of us with the richest ideas will create the greatest wealth in the world. Just think for a moment—you possess one of the most valuable and powerful pieces of equipment in the world right between your ears!

You have learned some powerful ways to run your own brain. The positive software that you have put into your mind will begin to manifest more and more beneficial results each day. The fact that you've chosen to invest in your own evolution sets you apart from the masses. It's a decision that will enrich the quality of your life many times over, because life is only as amazing as the way you choose to live it.

As you practice the techniques in this book, taking responsibility for programming your own mind, you are putting yourself at the forefront of our culture. You are becoming a leader, and the choices you make about where and how you lead will become increasingly significant.

As you continue on your journey to the life of your dreams, I would like to leave you with this Buddhist blessing:

May you be safe and protected

May you be happy and peaceful

May you be healthy and strong

May you carry your life with ease and grace

Until next we meet,

Paul McKenna

About the Author

Paul McKenna, PhD, is the best-selling author of *I Can Make You Thin* and *I Can Make You Sleep*. The London *Times* called him "one of the most important modern self-help gurus." Dr. McKenna has helped millions of people lose weight, quit smoking, overcome insomnia, eliminate stress, and increase self-confidence. He has appeared on *The Ellen DeGeneres Show, Rachael Ray, Good Morning America, The Early Show, The Dr. Oz Show, The Bonnie Hunt Show,* and *Fox and Friends*. His TV shows are regularly watched by hundreds of millions of people in forty-two countries around the world. His private clients include rock stars, movie stars, world champion athletes, and royalty. Now he wants to help you!

For more information about Paul McKenna
and his techniques, visit

WWW.MCKENNA.COM